M000317250

To

From

Date

Celebration Enterprises (CE)

UNSHAKEABLE: FACING YOUR GIANTS IN GOD'S STRENGTH

International Standard Book Number: 978-1-4675-6453-3

Copyright © 2022 Celebration Enterprises

Roswell, GA 30075
(678) 208-0736

Portions of this book were previously published in THE BEST OF THE WORD FOR YOU TODAY, Edition #6, ©2011 Celebration Enterprises, Inc. (ISBN # 978-0-578-08975-1) and THE BEST OF THE WORD FOR YOU TODAY, Edition #7, ©2014 Celebration Enterprises, Inc. (ISBN # 978-1-4951-0285-1) All Rights Reserved.

Scripture quotations marked (AMP) are taken from the *Amplified® Bible*. Copyright ©1954, 1958, 1962, 1964, 1965, 1987 by The Lockman Foundation. Used by permission *(www.lockman.org)*.

Scripture quotations marked (CEV) are from the *Contemporary English Version*. Copy- right ©1991, 1992, 1995 by American Bible Society. Used by permission.

Scripture quotations marked (GNT) are from the *Good News Translation in Today's English Version—Second Edition*. Copyright ©1992 by American Bible Society. Used by permission.

Scripture quotations marked (NAS) are taken from the *New American Standard Bible®*. Copyright ©1960, 1962, 1963, 1968, 1971, 1972, 1973, 1975, 1977, 1995, by The Lockman Foundation. Used by permission *(www.Lockman.org)*.

Scripture quotations marked (NCV) are taken from the *New Century Version®*. Copy- right ©2005 by Thomas Nelson, Inc. Used by permission. All rights reserved.

Scripture quotations marked (NIV) are taken from the Holy Bible, *New International Version®*, NIV®. Copyright ©1973, 1978, 1984 by Biblica, Inc.™ Used by Permission of Zondervan. All rights reserved worldwide, *(www.zondervan.com)*.

Scripture quotations marked (NKJV) are taken from the *New King James Version®*. Copyright ©1982 by Thomas Nelson, Inc. Used by permission. All rights reserved.

Scripture quotations marked (NLT) are taken from the *Holy Bible, New Living Translation*. Copyright ©1996, 2004, 2007. Used by permission of Tyndale House Publishers, Inc., Carol Stream, Illinois 60188. All rights reserved.

Scripture quotations marked (NRS) are taken from the *New Revised Standard Version of the Bible*. Copyright ©1952 [2nd editions, 1971] by the Division of Christian Education of the National Council of the Churches of Christ in the United States of America. Used by permission. All rights reserved.

Scripture quotations marked (PHPS) are taken from *The New Testament in Modern English*. Copyright ©1958, 1959, 1960 J.B. Phillips and 1947, 1952, 1955, 1957 The Macmillian Company, New York. Used by permission. All rights reserved.

Scripture quotations marked (TEV) are taken from *The Good News Bible, Today's English Version*. New York. American Bible Society, Copyright ©1992. Used by permission. All rights reserved.

Scripture quotations marked (TLB) are taken from *The Living Bible*. Copyright ©1997, 1971 by Tyndale House Publishers, Inc. Used by permission. All rights reserved.

Scripture quotations marked (TM) are taken from *The Message*. Copyright ©1993, 1994, 1995, 1996, 2000, 2001, 2002 by Eugene Peterson. Used by permission of Nav-Press Publishing Group.

Unmarked Scripture quotations are taken from the King James Version.

Printed in the United States of America. All rights reserved.

Under International Copyright Law, no part of this publication may be reproduced, stored, or transmitted by any means—electronic, mechanical, photographic (photo- copy), recording, or otherwise—without written permission from the Publisher.

A 90-DAY JOURNEY IN FAITH

UNSHAKEABLE

FACING YOUR GIANTS IN GOD'S STRENGTH

. . . .

BROUGHT TO YOU BY
THE WORD FOR YOU TODAY

SCRIPTURE TRANSLATIONS AND PARAPHRASES

This book utilizes several different translations and paraphrases. Why? First, the Bible was originally written using 11,280 Hebrew, Aramaic, and Greek words, but the typical English translation uses only around 6,000 words. Obviously, nuances and shades of meaning can be missed, so it is always helpful to compare translations. Second, we often miss the full impact of familiar Bible verses, not because of poor translating, but simply because they have become so familiar! Therefore, we have deliberately used paraphrases in order to help you see God's truth in new, fresh ways.

ABBREVIATIONS USED:

AMPC	The Amplified Bible (Classic)
CEV	Contemporary English Version
GNT	Good News Translation in Today's English Version
NAS	New American Standard
NCV	New Century Version
NIV	New International Version
NKJV	New King James Version
NLT	New Living Translation
NRS	New Revised Standard Version
TLB	The Living Bible
TM	The Message

All unnoted references are from the King James Version.

INTRODUCTION

What is the foundation of godly strength? Being unshakable in your faith. Through the storms you encounter, the obstacles that stand in your way, the depth of loss you experience, difficult circumstances that leave you hopeless, or the giants you face, your faith in God and His Word will keep you strong.

Your unshakable faith lays a firm foundation. It begins with your salvation and continues as you read and memorize Scripture, spend time daily in prayer, and seek God's will for your life.

In this volume, we'll take a look at the tenants of what makes an unshakable person. The entries are designed to encourage you in your journey so that you can become what God intends you to be—unshakable!

DAY 1

SEEING GOD IN YOUR EVERYDAY LIFE

When . . . he turned aside . . . God called to him.

EXODUS 3:4 NKJV

It was business-as-usual for Moses the day he noticed the burning bush, an event that wasn't uncommon in the hot desert. Except this time the bush kept burning. And "when . . . he turned aside to look, God called to him." You'll have some of your greatest spiritual experiences in the midst of your everyday life—if you're open to a divine interruption.

In Luke chapter ten, Mary ministered to Jesus' divine nature while Martha ministered to His human needs. But Martha's "kitchen agenda" made it almost impossible to interrupt her, while Mary was so heavenly minded she'd probably have forgotten to turn the stove on! Now, it takes both to achieve a balance. But if Jesus has to choose, He'll take foot-washers over master-chefs every time. That's because one of our primary focuses should always be praise and worship (expressed appreciation), resulting in greater intimacy with God.

Are you so busy working on your "to-do list" that it would take fire from heaven to get your attention? A well-known pastor writes: "You can be in the midst of a common moment, only this time the activity is filled with the presence of God. When in the middle of your harried day you notice something unusual . . . your first reaction might be, 'I'm too tired to investigate . . . I'm not going to disrupt my life.' Yet in that moment you may have the opportunity for a unique encounter with God. When you see the unusual in the midst of the mundane, don't continue business-as-usual. God may have ordained that moment to be life-changing for you and those around you."

GOD'S WORD FOR ME TODAY IS . . .

You'll have some of your greatest spiritual experiences in the midst of your everyday life.

DAY 2

BRING YOUR RED UMBRELLA

Ask . . . in prayer, believe that you have received it, and it will be yours.

MARK 11:24 NIV

When severe drought hit a small farming community in the Midwest, a local church called a prayer meeting and everybody showed up. Crisis has a way of getting our attention! As the pastor stood before his packed church he noticed an eleven-year-old girl sitting in the front row, beaming with excitement. Lying next to her was her bright red umbrella poised for use. The beauty and innocence of this sight made him smile as he compared the faith of this child with that of the rest of the people in the room. You see, the rest of them had just come to pray for rain—she had come to see God answer!

One of the dangers of praying, is praying, yet not really expecting anything: "Without faith it is impossible to please God, because anyone who comes to him must believe that . . . he rewards those who earnestly seek him" (Heb 11:6 NIV). You say, "So how do I get more faith?" By filling your mind with the Scriptures! "Faith cometh by hearing, and hearing by the word of God" (Ro 10:17). When you immerse yourself in God's Word an amazing thing happens: faith takes root and begins to grow. And faith is what makes your praying effective.

But what if your prayer lines up with God's Word, yet the answer is delayed? Keep praying and believing! "Do not throw away your confidence; it will be richly rewarded. You need to persevere so that when you have done the will of God, you will receive what he has promised" (Heb 10:35-36 NIV). So when you pray for rain, bring your "red umbrella!"

GOD'S WORD FOR ME TODAY IS . . .

When you immerse yourself in God's Word an amazing thing happens: faith takes root and begins to grow.

DAY 3

LET GOD NAME YOU

I will write on him the name of my God.

REVELATION 3:12 NIV

When Rachel the wife of Jacob was dying in childbirth, she named her son Benoni, meaning "Son of my sorrow." In the Bible, names were prophetic; they were given to forecast destiny. So after the funeral Jacob announced, "He shall not be called Benoni, son of my sorrow. He shall be called Benjamin, son of my right hand. He is my strength, not my sorrow!" And guess which name prevailed? Benjamin! You are who your Heavenly Father says you are. Try to remember that!

Maybe you're like Hananiah, Mishael and Azariah. If you don't know them perhaps you'll recognize them by the heathen names King Nebuchadnezzar gave them: Shadrach, "command of Aku;" Meshach, "pagan name;" and Abednego, "servant of Nego." These names expressed worship to heathen gods. The real names of the three Hebrew children, however, were Hananiah, "Jehovah is gracious;" Mishael, "Who is like God;" and Azariah, "Jehovah has helped." When the king threw them into the fiery furnace the names God called them prevailed. There's nothing like trouble to bring out your true identity! Aren't you glad you're not limited by public opinion? God's opinion will always prevail. The old king tried to change the name on the package, but he couldn't change the contents! Can you imagine these boys shouting when they came out of the fiery furnace? One would say, "Who is like God?" Another would lift his hands and shout, "Jehovah is gracious!" The other would smell his clothes, touch his hair and declare, "Jehovah has helped!" So stand up, step out, go forward in the name that God has given you!

GOD'S WORD FOR ME TODAY IS . . .

You're not limited by public opinion!

DAY 4

MEMORIZE THE SCRIPTURES

The word is near you, in your mouth and in your heart.

ROMANS 10:8 NKJV

Nothing pays greater spiritual dividends than memorizing Scripture. Your prayer life will be strengthened. Your witnessing will be more effective. Your counseling will be in demand. Your outlook will change. Your mind will become more alert. Your confidence will be enhanced. Your faith will be solidified. Even if you've tried memorizing Scripture and given up, try again using these seven simple steps: (1) Choose a time when your mind is free from outside distractions. (2) Learn the reference by repeating it every time you say the verse. Numbers are more difficult to remember than words. (3) Read each verse through several times—both in a whisper and aloud. Hearing yourself say the words helps cement them in your mind. (4) Break the passage into its natural phrases. Learn the reference, then the first phrase. Then repeat the reference and the first phrase as you go to the second phrase. Continue adding phrases one by one. (5) Learn a little bit perfectly, rather than a great deal poorly. Don't go on to the next verse until you can say the previous one perfectly. (6) Review the verse immediately. Twenty to thirty minutes later repeat what you've memorized. Before the day has ended, firmly fix the verse in your mind by going over it fifteen to twenty times. (You can do this while you're driving.) (7) Use the verse orally as soon as possible. The purpose of Scripture memorization is a practical one, not academic. Use the verse in conversation, in correspondence, in everyday opportunities. Relate what you've learned to your daily situation. You'll be thrilled with the results.

GOD'S WORD FOR ME TODAY IS . . .

Nothing pays greater spiritual dividends than memorizing Scripture.

DAY 5

P-R-A-Y!

Look to the Lord and his strength; seek his face always.

1 CHRONICLES 16:11 NIV

To help you remember the four parts of prayer, think of the acrostic P-R-A-Y: P—Praise the Lord! Not sure how? Think you'll run out of words? Not if you use the Scriptures. David gives us a beautiful example in 1 Ch 29:11-13. It's one you can use: "Yours, O Lord, is the greatness and the power and the glory and the majesty and the splendor . . . Yours, O Lord, is the kingdom . . . In your hands are strength and power to exalt and give strength to all. Now, our God, we give you thanks, and praise your glorious name." R—Repent of your sins! Just as heat forces impurities to the surface so the metal refiner can remove them, your prayer time will reveal attitudes that must be changed, habits that must be broken, and barriers to blessing that must be removed. It's not enough to tell God about your sins. He already knows them. You must ask Him to help you turn away from them. This is true repentance. A—Ask for yourself and others! Your prayers invite God into the situation, and your faith activates His power to change it. There's no distance in prayer, no culture or language barrier it can't overcome. It's like throwing on a power switch—things begin to move when we pray. Jesus said, "I will give you the keys of the Kingdom of Heaven . . . whatever doors you open on earth shall be open in heaven" (Mt 16:19 TLB). Y—Yield yourself to God's will! Declaring the Lordship of Jesus Christ in your life is like signing your name to the bottom of a blank check, and inviting Him to fill in the amount.

GOD'S WORD FOR ME TODAY IS . . .

"In your hands are strength and power to exalt and give strength to all. Now, our God, we give you thanks, and praise your glorious name."

DAY 6

GROWING STRONG ROOTS

May your roots go down deep into the soil of God's marvelous love.

EPHESIANS 3:17 TLB

Philip Gulley writes: "Growing up I had an old neighbor named Dr. Gibbs. When he wasn't saving lives he was planting trees. The good doctor had some interesting theories on plant husbandry. He came from the 'no pain, no gain' school of horticulture. He never watered his new trees. He said watering plants spoiled them; if you water them, each successive generation will grow weaker. So you have to make things tough for them and weed out the weenie trees early on. He talked about how watering trees made for shallow roots, and how trees that weren't watered had to grow deep roots in search of moisture. He'd plant an oak, and instead of watering it, every morning he'd beat it with a rolled-up newspaper. Smack! Slap! Pow! He said it made the trees pay attention. Dr. Gibbs went to glory a couple of years after I left home. Every now and again I'd walk by his house and look at those trees he planted twenty-five years ago. They are granite strong, big and robust. They wake up every morning and beat their chests and drink their coffee black. I planted a couple of trees a few years back. Carried water to them for a solid summer, sprayed them, prayed over them. Three years of coddling has resulted in trees that expect to be waited on hand and foot. Whenever a cold wind blows in, they tremble. Sissy trees. Funny thing about those trees of Dr. Gibbs. Adversity seems to have benefited them in ways comfort and ease never could."

GOD'S WORD FOR ME TODAY IS . . .

Adversity can be beneficial in ways comfort and ease never can.

DAY 7

FAITH (1)

With God on our side . . . how can we lose?

ROMANS 8:31 TM

Faith is like a muscle; opposition may strain it, but in the end it grows stronger. The Psalmist David understood this principle. He was continually hounded by his enemies. Even when he was being anointed to sit on the throne, Saul the old king was still occupying it. But instead of losing faith in God's promise, David understood that "the Lord has set apart [earmarked] the godly man for Himself" (Ps 4:3 NAS). So he declared, "In peace I will . . . lie down . . . For You . . . Lord, make me to dwell in safety" (Ps 4:8 NAS). When the Philistines captured him he prayed, "When I am afraid, I will . . . trust in You" (Ps 56:3 NAS). And when he ended up in a cave while fleeing from Saul's jealous rage he said, "I will hide beneath the shadow of your wings until this . . . is past" (Ps 57:1 TLB).

During the third century, when St. Felix of Nola was running from his enemies, he took refuge in an abandoned building. Eventually a spider began to weave a web across the door, sealing it off and making it look like nobody had been inside for months. As a result his pursuers passed by and didn't bother looking there. Later, stepping out into the sunshine, Felix declared, "Where God is, a spider's web is a wall. And where He isn't, a wall is but a spider's web." Jesus said you'd have problems on earth; people will disappoint you, and you'll disappoint yourself. Sometimes you'll end up in trouble because of something you did, and other times because of circumstances you have no control over. But God is with you either way. And like Paul said, "With God on our side . . . how can we lose?"

GOD'S WORD FOR ME TODAY IS . . .

Faith is like a muscle; opposition may strain it, but in the end it grows stronger.

DAY 8

FAITH (2)

Job . . . fell to the ground and worshiped.

JOB 1:20 NIV

Every day God sends us opportunities for spiritual growth—disguised as problems. Nowhere is this more evident than in the life of Job the patriarch. After losing his house, his children, his livestock, and his health, the Bible says, "Job . . . fell to the ground and worshiped." That's not the normal human response to tragedy, is it? Job didn't react that way because he understood everything that was happening to him. No, he bowed in worship in spite of his circumstances! He was able to respond that way because: (a) He looked up! In the midst of his troubles, Job saw the God who promised to direct each step we take. More importantly, he trusted God's heart of love and recognized His sovereign right to decide all things. (b) He looked forward! He reminded himself that in the final analysis God will make everything right for us. (c) He looked inside! He knew that God was teaching him something valuable through this experience: "When He has tried me, I shall come forth as gold" (Job 23:10 NAS). Like clay in the hands of the potter, Job decided to trust God.

That kind of thinking was no easier for him than it is for you. Our human nature always wants to cling to the familiar and return to the safety of yesterday, even though we know it's not where God wants us. The fears, surprises and adversity that lie around the bend make us want to cut and run. But if you do you'll short-circuit God's plan for your life. So what should you do? "Stand . . . still, and see the salvation [deliverance] of the Lord" (2Ch 20:17), because trust always leads to deliverance.

GOD'S WORD FOR ME TODAY IS . . .

***Trust** always leads to **deliverance**.*

DAY 9

FAITH (3)

When we trust . . . him, we're free . . . to go wherever we need.

EPHESIANS 3:12 TM

When you walk by faith God will test you—like He tested Elijah! The prophet was sitting alone beside a dried-up stream when God sent him on a 100-mile hike through the desert to Zarephath. And at the time Elijah was a wanted man, so coming out of hiding meant really trusting God for his safety. Next, God told him that when he got there an impoverished widow would provide for him—a humbling prospect for a leader who's used to ministering to others. Elijah found the widow in the middle of a famine, cooking her last meal. Her circumstances looked grim. But he challenged her to obey God, promising: "There will always be flour and olive oil . . . in your containers until . . . the Lord sends rain and the crops grow" (1 Ki 17:14 NLT). What gave Elijah the faith to say that? Because he'd personally proven God's faithfulness throughout his own life! You can talk that way when you walk that way!

Rubbing shoulders with people who trust God is contagious; it builds your faith. And this woman was no exception. She and her son may not have eaten gourmet meals every night, but God made sure that as long as the famine lasted they had all they needed. So if you don't have everything you want right now, honor God with what you've got, and trust Him that when the time is right He'll send an increase. Paul says: "When we trust . . . him, we're free . . . to go wherever we need." If God is directing you to your own personal "Zarephath," or anywhere else that doesn't make sense to you right now, don't argue. Go, because His promises hinge on your obedience.

GOD'S WORD FOR ME TODAY IS . . .

Rubbing shoulders with people who trust God is contagious; it builds your faith.

DAY 10

FAITH (4)

Faith is the reason we remember great people.

HEBREWS 11:2 NCV

When the Bible says, "Faith is the reason we remember great people," maybe you think you would never qualify to march in that parade. You might be surprised; listen to some of the people God singles out in Hebrews chapter eleven.

Noah was a farmer-turned-boat-builder who got his name in lights because the boat he built survived a universal flood. What we sometimes overlook is that afterwards he got blind drunk and disgraced his family. Abraham wasn't a prophet or a teacher; he was a businessman with a character flaw who tried to save his neck by lying and compromising his wife's safety. Sarah, a homemaker, laughed when God told her she'd give birth to a child at ninety years old (and you'd probably have done the same!). There's Joseph, a slave with a prison record, who ended up becoming Prime Minister. Then there's Rahab the harlot; how did somebody with her background ever become a woman of faith? You'll have to ask God; He included her on the list. And how about Jacob the con artist: would you like to do business with him? Of course there was David, whose womanizing led to murder. And what about Gideon and Samuel, two spiritual leaders whose children went astray?

The bottom line is, all these "greats" were human just like us. In fact some of them would make us look like saints! You won't find any stained-glass material in this chapter. They faltered, fumbled the ball, and went through hard times. Their only distinction is—they believed God and He honored their faith!

GOD'S WORD FOR ME TODAY IS . . .

Believe God and He will honor your faith.

DAY 11

GET ON THE BUS!

Therefore, my dear brothers, stand firm. Let nothing move you.

1 CORINTHIANS 15:58 NIV

Patsy Clairmont writes: "Jason, our youngest, has two goals in life. One is to have fun; the other is to rest. And he does both quite well. So I shouldn't have been surprised about what happened when I sent him to school one fall day. As Jason headed off for the bus I busied myself, preparing for a full day. The knock on the door was a surprise, and disruptive to my morning rhythm, which is not something I have a lot of. I flew to the door, jerked it open, only to find myself looking at Jason. 'What are you doing here?' I demanded. 'I've quit school,' he announced. 'Quit school?' I repeated in disbelief and at a decibel too high for human ears, swallowing once, and trying to remember some motherly psychology. But all that came to my mind was 'a stitch in time saves nine' and 'starve a fever, feed a cold,' or something like that. Somehow they didn't seem to apply to a six-year-old dropout dilemma. So I questioned 'Why have you quit school?' Without hesitation he proclaimed, 'It's too long, it's too hard, and it's too boring!' 'Jason,' I instantly retorted, 'You have just described life. Get on the bus!'"

When it comes to the Christian life, God promises no bed of roses on the battlefield and no carpet on the racetrack, just a checkerboard of adversity and advancement! His Word says: "Stand firm. Let nothing move you. Always give yourselves fully to the work of the Lord, because you know that your labor in the Lord is not in vain." So the word for you today is—get on the bus!

GOD'S WORD FOR ME TODAY IS . . .

God promises no bed of roses on the battlefield and no carpet on the racetrack, just a checkerboard of adversity and advancement!

DAY 12

PEACE "IN SPITE OF"

You will experience God's peace, which is far more wonderful than the human mind can understand.

PHILIPPIANS 4:7 TLB

Catherine Marshall writes: "A king once offered a prize to the artist who could paint the best picture of peace. Many tried, but there were only two the king really liked. One was of a calm lake. It was a perfect mirror for the peaceful towering mountains all around it. Overhead was a blue sky with fluffy white clouds. The other picture had mountains too. But they were rugged and bare. Above them was an angry sky from which fell rain, and in which lightning played. Down the side of the mountains tumbled a waterfall. This did not look peaceful at all. But when the king looked closely he saw behind the waterfall a tiny bush growing in a crack in the rock. In the bush a mother bird had built her nest. There, in spite of the rush of angry water, she sat on her nest—in perfect peace. Which picture do you think won the prize? The king chose the second picture. Why? 'Because,' explained the king, 'Peace does not mean to be in a place where there is no noise, trouble or hard work. Peace means to be in the middle of all these things and still be calm in your heart.'"

At some point we all discover that there's no safe harbor free from storms; that peace is not the absence of storms, but: (a) the assurance of God's presence and protection in the midst of them; (b) the growth of our faith and character because of them; (c) His rock-solid promise to bring us through them stronger and wiser.

GOD'S WORD FOR ME TODAY IS . . .

Peace is having calm in your heart in the midst of trouble.

DAY 13

ASK GOD FOR WHAT YOU WANT!

The reason you don't have what you want is . . . you don't ask God.

JAMES 4:2 TLB

Imagine walking into a restaurant on a whim and asking if your order is ready. "When did you call it in?" the server asks. "Oh I didn't," you reply, "I just thought perhaps you'd have something with my name on it." Sound ridiculous? No more so than expecting God to answer requests you haven't made—or have made without faith. James says: "The reason you don't have what you want is . . . you don't ask God." Does that mean He'll automatically give you everything you ask for? No. James adds: "Even when you do ask you don't get it because . . . you want only what will give you pleasure" (v. 3 TLB). Your motives need to be in tune with what God knows is best for you. John says, "This is the confidence . . . we have in Him . . . if we ask anything . . . according to His will . . . He . . . hears" (1Jn 5:14 AMP).

Lamentations 3:25 says: "The Lord is good to those who wait . . . expectantly for Him" (AMP). Expectant prayer demonstrates confidence in God's goodness. Instead of fretting and taking matters into your own hands, when you say, "Lord, I'm going to trust You with this, regardless of the outcome," He'll honor your faith. Paul says: "Pray and ask God for everything you need, always giving thanks" (Php 4:6 NCV). Do you need a job? Help overcoming a problem? Salvation for your loved ones? A deeper walk with God? Physical or emotional healing? Jesus said: "It gives your Father great happiness to give you the [benefits of his] Kingdom" (Lk 12:32 NLT). God wants to be good to you, so tell Him the "desires of your heart" (Ps 37:4 NKJV). And thank Him that the answer will come—in His time!

GOD'S WORD FOR ME TODAY IS . . .

Expectant prayer demonstrates confidence in God's goodness.

DAY 14

FAITH VS. CONTROL

If you give up your life for me, you will save it.

LUKE 9:24 CEV

When you obsess over problems instead of looking to God for solutions, the Enemy will magnify your fears. If he can't get you to worry about the present he'll remind you of everything that could go wrong in the future! Ralph Waldo Emerson said, "All I have seen, has taught me to trust God for all I haven't seen." The last time you checked, wasn't God still bigger than any terrorist attack, financial disaster, illness, accusation, or mess you found yourself in? Well, He hasn't changed! The Psalmist said, "He won't go to sleep . . . The Lord is . . . at your right side . . . [He] will . . . keep you safe . . . wherever you go" (Ps 121:3-8 CEV); plus His angels are watching over you 24/7.

It all comes down to faith vs. control. You can struggle to handle things on your own—or trust your heavenly Father. That's the choice! It's not about "blind faith," it's about believing that God is who He says He is. And it's an issue you need to settle in your mind once and for all, because if you don't believe He wants only the best for you, you'll keep trying to run the show. Control isn't responsibility. Responsibility is doing your part by praying, obeying, and trusting God. Control is manipulating the circumstances to engineer the outcome you want. Jesus knows how we like holding on to things we're not wise enough to control, so He said: "If you want to save your life, you will destroy it. But if you give up your life for me, you will save it." Bottom line—you either trust God or you don't!

GOD'S WORD FOR ME TODAY IS . . .

You can struggle to handle things on your own—or trust your heavenly Father.

DAY 15

'GO!'

I'll take the hand of those who don't know the way . . . to show them what roads to take.

ISAIAH 42:16 TM

Are you facing a situation that feels overwhelming and you're afraid to make a wrong move? Or maybe you're saying no to something in your life that you'd really like to say yes to. A well-known counselor says: "For years I heard about hiking. It sounded elusive, difficult . . . and mysterious. When a friend asked me to go hiking . . . I began thinking . . . what if I couldn't do it well enough? Or I didn't know how to do it at all? 'Don't be ridiculous,' I scolded myself. 'You're making this more complicated than it is . . . it's just walking, and you've been doing that since you were a baby!' We left . . . and I followed . . . as he started up a steep incline. 'Just walk,' I told myself . . . 'Put one foot in front of another . . . like you've done all your life.' I didn't make it to the top of the mountain that day, but I made it halfway . . . Start where you are. Start poorly. Just start . . . if you already knew how to do it well, it wouldn't be a lesson . . . and you'd never have the thrill of victory, years from now looking back."

God has promised to "take the hand of those who don't know the way . . . to show them what roads to take." You say, "But what if I get into difficulty?" You probably will! But God says: "When you're in over your head, I'll be there with you" (Isa 43:2 TM). But you've got to be willing to "go" in order for God to bring you "through!" In other words—you have to be willing to get your feet wet. The thing to keep in mind is: "God . . . goes ahead of you" (Dt 1:30 TM).

GOD'S WORD FOR ME TODAY IS . . .

You have to be willing to get your feet wet.

DAY 16

WALKING THE PLANK!

Don't be afraid . . . I am with you.

ISAIAH 41:10 NLT

It's easy to walk across a plank that's on the ground, but raise it a little and it becomes harder. Now, imagine that same plank 100 feet up, without a safety net under it; looks scary, doesn't it? The Bible says, "Fear is crippling" (1Jn 4:18 TM). And the more that's at stake the harder it is; white-knuckle syndrome kicks in and you develop a case of the "what ifs." Fear is living in the future before you get there. And among the trolls lurking under the bridge to your future, inspirational speaker Dr. Joan Borysenko cites two things: (1) Fear of failure. She writes: "When I was admitted to Harvard, I was sure there'd been a computer error and that I'd be exposed as a fraud. A lawyer friend of mine stops short of terror every time she has to give a final argument before a jury. Even when you're an expert fear doesn't necessarily go away. Accepting fear as part of the journey instead of running from it helps you conquer it! (2) Fear of imperfection. This one makes it hard to do anything, because perfectionists set unattainable goals and berate themselves when they can't reach them. It's impossible to learn without making mistakes; so learn, and move on."

God says: "Don't be afraid . . . I am with you," so ask yourself what He wants and stop worrying about people pleasing. Solomon said, "Fear of human opinion disables [you]" (Pr 29:25 TM). When you look back at what you've already overcome, you begin to realize that most times failure doesn't do permanent damage—you actually grow through it! So stay focused; with God, you can walk any plank. Who knows, you might even begin to enjoy the challenge!

GOD'S WORD FOR ME TODAY IS . . .

*With God, you can walk **any** plank.*

DAY 17

OVERCOME YOUR PAST!

Forgetting those things which are behind.

PHILIPPIANS 3:13

It's impossible to succeed in life without overcoming your past. When the great Paderewski first started to study piano his teacher told him his hands were too small to master the keyboard. Yet the fire in his soul drove him to become a world-renowned pianist. When Enrico Caruso first started to study voice his teacher said he sounded like the wind whistling through the window. Today Caruso is remembered as one of the world's greatest tenors. If you need inspiration to overcome your life's obstacles, look no further than Christ. Society called His birth illegitimate. He was born into a hated minority who experienced brutal oppression every day. The recognized church branded Him a heretic. The state called Him an insurrectionist too dangerous to live. One of His closest friends betrayed Him to enrich himself. He was sentenced without a fair trial and died like a common criminal. And what was His response to His suffering, and ours? "Be of good cheer; I have overcome the world" (Jn 16:33).

We spend far too much time crying over spilt milk. Rather than giving attention to the most important assignment we have every morning—our choice of an attitude—we waste our time and energy on things that cannot be changed. You cannot change the death of a loved one. You cannot change the fact that one day your spouse told you, "I want a divorce." The past is over. Look forward. Press on! God says, "The plans I have for you . . . are . . . good" (Jer 29:11 NLT). That means the best is yet to be!

GOD'S WORD FOR ME TODAY IS . . .

Look forward. Press on!

DAY 18

YOU CAN'T ESCAPE THIS TRIAL!

Consider it all joy . . . when you encounter various trials.

JAMES 1:2 NAS

The Bible doesn't tell us to rejoice when we mess up and get into trouble. God can certainly use our mistakes to teach us, but that's not what James has in mind. Some of our trials just come from "living." Things aren't going right. Usually it's not one big thing but a lot of little things. We encounter physical, financial, relational or emotional trials that knock us for a loop. Peter calls this "the trial of your faith" (1Pe 1:7). What's on trial? Your faith! Whatever the size or length of our trial, there's nowhere we can go to escape the trial of our faith. Trying to avoid it is like changing schools in hopes of avoiding a test you don't want to take. But the next school will have tests too, probably harder than the ones in the school you just left, and now you're that much further behind in your studies and preparation. You can't outrun God-ordained trials. He knows where to find you!

The good news is, there's no such thing as a purposeless trial! Each trial is designed to launch us to a new spiritual level. The interesting thing about our trials is, they're custom made; they have our name on them. Paul discovered two things about his trials: (a) The reason for the trial. "To keep me from becoming conceited" (2Co 12:7 NIV). (b) The result of the trial. "That Christ's power may rest on me" (v. 9 NIV). Like a tailor measuring you for a suit that will fit perfectly, the Holy Spirit customizes the trials we encounter to meet our spiritual need, to mold us, and to make us more like Jesus!

GOD'S WORD FOR ME TODAY IS . . .

God knows where to find you!

DAY 19

KEEP PERSEVERING!

Blessed is the man who perseveres.

JAMES 1:12 NIV

On June 1, 1965, a thirteen-foot boat slipped quietly out of Falmouth, Massachusetts. Its destination? Falmouth, England. It would be the smallest craft ever to make the voyage. Its name? Tinkerbelle. Its pilot? Robert Manry, a copy editor for the Cleveland Plain Dealer newspaper who felt that ten years at a desk was enough boredom for anyone. Manry was afraid, not of the ocean but of all the people who would try to talk him out of the trip. So he only shared it with some relatives and his wife Virginia, his greatest source of support. The trip? He spent harrowing nights of sleeplessness trying to cross shipping lanes without getting run over. Weeks at sea caused his food to become tasteless. Loneliness led to hallucinations. His rudder broke three times. Storms swept him overboard. Had it not been for the rope around his waist he would never have been able to pull himself back on board. Finally, after seventy-eight days alone at sea he sailed into Falmouth, England. During those nights at the tiller he had fantasized about what he would do once he arrived. He expected to simply check into a hotel, eat dinner alone, then next morning see if perhaps the Associated Press might be interested in his story. What a surprise! Word had spread far and wide. To his amazement, three hundred vessels with horns blasting escorted Tinkerbelle into port. And 47,000 people stood screaming and cheering him to the shore.

One of the great themes of Scripture is perseverance. No matter how great your calling, your talent, your cause or your goal, without perseverance you won't make it. Hence James writes, "Blessed is the man who perseveres."

GOD'S WORD FOR ME TODAY IS . . .

Without perseverance you won't make it.

DAY 20

"GET OVER IT!"

In every thing give thanks.

1 THESSALONIANS 5:18

Consider Moses, the lawgiver and liberator to whom God gave the Ten Commandments. His name is still known all over the earth 4,000 years after his death. But remember, this same Moses was a murderer. He was listed in Egypt as public enemy number one. He was a fugitive from justice who fled to the wilderness where he lived for forty years as a shepherd. Yet with the chisel of adversity God was shaping Moses to stand in Pharaoh's majestic palace and announce, "Let my people go!" A nation was born because this man refused to stop struggling to achieve his divine destiny.

Don't be paralyzed by your past. If God used Moses, He'll use you. Everyone goes through adversity. The phrase to remember when things go wrong is: "Get over it!" Have you been hurt? Get over it! Have you been betrayed? Get over it! Have you failed? Get over it! Paul writes: "In every thing give thanks." In reversal, give thanks. In heartache, give thanks. In poverty and in prosperity, give thanks. God is greater than the criticism you're getting. He's greater than the giants you're facing. He's greater than the mountain you're climbing. He's greater than the burdens you're carrying. Look at the Bible record of men and women who chose to focus on the silver lining, not the dark cloud. These people didn't curse the darkness, they shone a light and scattered it. They chose the right attitude, an attitude of faith. Come on, stop hiding from success because you're afraid to fail. Failure means you're a learner, not a loser. Stop fearing risk! Take God's hand, step out and fulfill His purpose for your life.

GOD'S WORD FOR ME TODAY IS . . .

God is greater than the giants you're facing, the mountain you're climbing, and the burdens you're carrying.

DAY 21

TESTIFYING WITHOUT A TOUCH

Blessed are those who believe without seeing.

JOHN 20:29 NLT

Asking for proof before you believe something can stop you from receiving what God wants you to accept based on His Word. Thomas watched Jesus die. That's hard evidence to refute. As a result Thomas decided to believe only what he could see and verify. When your faith's been shaken you're inclined to cling to things that are practical, absolute and tangible. Jesus graciously gave Thomas the proof he needed, and said: "You believe because you have seen . . . Blessed are those who believe without seeing." The fact remains, however, if Thomas hadn't been permitted to see and touch Jesus, it wouldn't have changed the reality of the Resurrection one iota. Thomas' problem wasn't lack of faith, it was misdirected faith. He trusted only what he could process on a human level. Sound familiar?

By contrast, when Mary Magdalene met Jesus at the tomb He told her, "Don't touch me . . . But go find my brothers and tell them" (v. 17 TLB). Mary once washed Jesus' feet with her tears and dried them with her hair; touch was important to her. And touching Jesus at that moment would have confirmed what she'd seen and heard. This time, however, Jesus asked her to trust His Word and not His flesh; to be willing to testify without a touch. It's wonderful when we "feel the touch of God" calming us, strengthening us, reassuring us He's still in control. The truth is, His touch has often kept us from giving up or going over the edge. But sometimes He asks us to trust Him without the crutch of sensory perception, to testify without a touch. That's faith at its highest level.

GOD'S WORD FOR ME TODAY IS . . .

God is still in control!

DAY 22

TAKE COURAGE

Act with courage, and may the Lord be with those who do well.

2 CHRONICLES 19:11 NIV

One of the last obstacles between Israel and the Promised Land was the River Jordan. But God had a plan. He told the priests carrying the Ark that when they stepped in the river, the waters would roll back. There are two important lessons here for you: (1) Nothing happens until you quit holding back! You can't wait for everything to be perfect. You can't wait until your fear subsides. You must take the initiative. Overcomers understand that momentum is your friend. As soon as you start moving forward, certain things become clearer and easier. And when the momentum gets strong enough, many of the problems actually take care of themselves. Maybe you've heard the story of the tourist in a small town who asked an old man, "Can you tell me something this town is noted for?" After a moment's hesitation he replied, "Well, you can start here and go anywhere in the world you want." That's true of you too. Where you finish in life isn't determined so much by where you start, as by whether you start. If you're willing to get started, there's no telling how far you'll go. (2) You must be willing to persevere. The Jordan River didn't dry up the moment the priests stepped into it. God dried it up twenty-six miles upstream, so they had to wait till all that water passed by (See Jos 3:14-17). Why did God do it that way? Because He sees the big picture. God planned an opening wide enough for not just one or two, but for more than a million people to cross. So trust God, and take the initiative!

GOD'S WORD FOR ME TODAY IS . . .

If you're willing to get started, there's no telling how far you'll go.

DAY 23

NO FEAR

Do not be afraid . . . The Lord . . . is going before you.

DEUTERONOMY 1:29-30 NIV

Notice two things about taking the initiative: (1) Taking the initiative closes the door to fear. We all have fears. The question is, are we going to control them or allow them to control us? Norman Vincent Peale said: "Action is a great restorer and builder of confidence. Inaction is not only the result, but the cause of fear. Perhaps the action you take will be successful; perhaps different action or adjustments will have to follow. But any action is better than no action at all." To have any chance at getting what we desire, we need to work for it. Nothing is as discouraging or draining as hanging on to an uncompleted task. The longer we let things slide, the harder they become. The hardest work is often the accumulation of many easy things that should have been done yesterday, last week or last month. The way to get rid of a difficult task is—do it! (2) Taking the initiative opens the door to opportunity. People who take the initiative and work hard may succeed, or fail. But anyone who doesn't take initiative is guaranteed to fail! So, ask God, "Is there a decision I should be making? Is there a problem I should be solving? Is there a project I should be starting? Is there a goal I should be setting or striving toward? Is there an opportunity I should be seizing?" Solomon writes: "If you wait for perfect conditions, you will never get anything done" (Ecc 11:4 TLB). It's better to be 80 percent sure, and start, than to wait until you're 100 percent sure, because by then the opportunity may have passed you by.

GOD'S WORD FOR ME TODAY IS . . .

Any action is better than no action at all.

53

DAY 24

FAITH AND CAREFUL PLANNING

We should make plans—counting on God to direct us.

PROVERBS 16:9 TLB

There must be a balance between faith and careful planning. Yet, talk to some professing Christians and you might think otherwise. For example, talk with some who are unemployed and they'll tell you, "I'm just waiting for the Lord to provide a job." That's fine, but have you sharpened your job skills? And where have you placed your résumé? You say, "I'm not going that route; I'm just waiting on God." Oh, really? Then you won't mind going hungry for a while. The old motto of soldiers during the Revolutionary War applies here: "Trust God, but keep your powder dry!" Place your life in God's hands, but stay at the ready. You must do all you can to prepare yourself, understanding that the favor you need comes from the Lord.

To walk by faith does not mean you stop thinking, planning, taking advice, and self-correcting. And it definitely doesn't imply becoming lazy or apathetic. What a distortion of biblical faith! Trust God for your finances, but don't "blow your budget." Trust God for safety in the car, but don't pass on a blind curve. Trust God for your health, but don't chain-smoke, stay up half the night and subsist on potato chips and carbonated drinks. Acting foolishly, expecting God to bail you out when things go amiss, isn't faith, it's presumption. Wisdom says do all you can, then trust God to do what you cannot do. Faith and careful planning go hand-in-hand. They always have and they always will!

GOD'S WORD FOR ME TODAY IS . . .

Wisdom says do all you can, then trust God to do what you cannot do.

DAY 25

WHEN YOU LOSE WHAT YOU LOVE

When they walk through the Valley of Weeping . . . They will continue to grow stronger.

PSALM 84:6-7 NLT

When you lose what you love you go through five stages: (1) Denial—"No, it can't be happening." (2) Anger—"God, why are You permitting this?" (3) Bargaining—"Please make it go away." (4) Depression—Silence and withdrawal. (5) Acceptance—"Not my will but Thine be done." Whether it's the loss of a child, a marriage, a job, your health, or your spouse, when you turn to God He'll give you the grace to embrace it, grieve it, express it, release it, and go on to become stronger. Sometimes we seek quick relief by releasing it before we've gone through these stages. That's because we fear the process. We've been taught that any show of emotion is a show of weakness, so we stuff it. But we only stuff it into our emotional garbage can, then spend all our time and energy sitting on the lid, trying to keep the contents from spilling out. "You shall know the truth, and the truth shall make you free" (Jn 8:32 NKJV). It's knowing and embracing the truth, including its painful aspects, that sets you free. You must be willing to forgive. But until you come to grips with the enormity of your loss, including any injustice of what was done to you, you are not ready to forgive. When you rush to forgive, you forgive only in part and you're released only in part. Are you running from pain today? Are you trading it in prematurely for some other feeling? That's not God's way. Jesus said, "You will weep and mourn . . . but [eventually] your grief will turn to joy . . . and no one will take [it] away" (Jn 16:20-22 NIV).

GOD'S WORD FOR ME TODAY IS . . .

It's knowing and embracing the truth, including its painful aspects, that sets you free.

DAY 26

READ YOUR BIBLE (1)

If ye continue in my word, then are ye my disciples indeed.

JOHN 8:31

You cannot be a disciple of Jesus without a regular intake of God's Word. Jesus said, "If ye continue in my word, then are ye my disciples indeed." This word "continue" means to live each day by its principles. The story's told of a man who came to pick up his wife after church: "Is the sermon over?" he asked. A turned-on member replied, "No, it has just begun. Now the rest is up to us!"

The common denominator of every great man and woman of God in history is that they disciplined themselves to spend regular time with the Lord in His Word. What made George Muller so successful? During his lifetime he read through the Bible over two hundred times—and more than half of those readings on his knees, praying over the Word while studying it. When you know God that well, you'll pray specifically and get specific answers. Most of us who say we believe the Bible from cover to cover—have never read it from cover to cover! We are more faithful to the advice columnists and the sports pages of the newspaper than we are to God's Word. People who are not professing Christians wouldn't dream of leaving their homes in the morning until they've read their horoscope. Imagine what would happen if you committed yourself with equal vigor to reading your Bible before you leave for work, school, or wherever? It would change your life, and impact those around you! So, read your Bible!

GOD'S WORD FOR ME TODAY IS . . .

Commit yourself with vigor to reading your Bible.

DAY 27

READ YOUR BIBLE (2)

Continue in . . . the Holy Scriptures, which are able to make you wise.

2 TIMOTHY 3:14-15 NKJV

Why don't we read God's Word more? Three reasons: (1) We don't know how! We hear the pastor preach a great sermon and think, "Why didn't I see that?" Because the pastor spends hours praying over it and studying the Scriptures; we don't! (2) We're not motivated! That's because we haven't experienced the joy that comes from personally discovering great truths from God's Word. We've become satisfied with getting what we need from somebody else rather than finding it out for ourselves. Understand this: If you ever get serious about studying the Bible on your own, you'll never fully be satisfied with a secondhand knowledge of the Scriptures. Dr. Paul Lyttle once compared personal Bible study to eating peanuts: "Once you start doing it, you're hooked! When you discover how good Bible study 'tastes' you'll find yourself going back for more and more. Yes, personal Bible study can be habit-forming!" (3) We are lazy! Bible study is hard work. There are no shortcuts to it. It takes time, effort, concentration and persistence. Most of its great truths don't lie on the surface; we have to dig for them. Dr. Howard Hendricks describes the three stages of Bible study: (a) The "castor oil" stage—we study the Bible because we know it's good for us, but it's not too enjoyable. (b) The "cereal" stage—our Bible study is dry and uninteresting, but we know it's nourishing. (c) The "peaches and cream" stage—we are really feasting on the Word of God. Bottom line? "Continue in . . . the Holy Scriptures, which are able to make you wise."

GOD'S WORD FOR ME TODAY IS . . .

Take time to experience the joy that comes from personally discovering great truths from God's Word.

DAY 28

FIND YOUR STRENGTH ZONE

He alone decides which gift each person should have.

1 CORINTHIANS 12:11 NLT

We all have equal value in God's eyes, but we don't have equal giftedness. In their book Now, Discover Your Strengths, Marcus Buckingham and Donald O. Clifton state that every person is capable of doing something better than the next 10,000 people. And they support that with research. They call this area your strength zone, and they encourage you to find it and make the most of it. It doesn't matter how aware you are of your abilities, how you feel about yourself, or whether you have previously achieved success. You have talent, and God requires you to develop it! But you can only develop the talent you have, not the one you want. When it comes to your character, you must never stop working on your areas of weakness. But when it comes to fulfilling your God-given assignment, you must recognize your strength zone and give yourself to it. Dr. John Maxwell writes: "It's been my observation that people can increase their ability in an area by only two points on a scale of 1-10. For example, if your natural talent in an area is 4, with hard work you may raise it to a 6. In other words, you can go from a little below average to a little above average. But let's say you find a place where you are a 7; you have the potential to become a 9, maybe even a 10, if it's your strength zone and you work hard! That helps you advance from 1 in 10,000 talent to 1 in 100,000 talent—but only if you do the other things needed to maximize your talent." So, find your strength zone!

GOD'S WORD FOR ME TODAY IS . . .

You have talent, and God requires you to develop it!

DAY 29

THE SPIRIT OF CALEB

My servant Caleb has a different spirit.

NUMBERS 14:24 NIV

Caleb wasn't into "safe living." As a young man he came back from the Promised Land, stood with the minority and announced, "With God on our side we'll take it!" At eighty-five, he was still slaying giants and claiming mountains. That's because he had "a different spirit." He wasn't a "go with the flow and expect the status quo" guy. Richard Edler writes: "Safe living generally makes for regrets later on. We are all given talents and dreams. Sometimes the two don't seem to match. But usually we compromise both before ever finding out. Later on, we find ourselves looking back longingly to that time when we should have chased our true dreams and our true talents for all they were worth. Don't let yourself be pressured into thinking that your dreams or your talents aren't prudent. They were never meant to be prudent. They were meant to bring joy and fulfillment into your life." If a caterpillar refuses to get into its cocoon it'll never transform and will be forever relegated to crawling on the ground, even though it had the potential to fly.

What do you believe God's called you to do? Do it! God's not limited by your IQ, He's limited by your "I can't." The poet said: "If you think you are beaten, you are. If you think you dare not, you don't. If you'd like to win but you think you can't, it's almost certain you won't. Life's battles don't always go to the stronger or faster man, but sooner or later the man who wins, is the man who believes he can." The spirit of Caleb is the "can do" spirit! Have you got it?

GOD'S WORD FOR ME TODAY IS . . .

Your dreams are meant to bring joy and fulfillment into your life.

DAY 30

"NEVERTHELESS . . ."

Nevertheless David took the stronghold of Zion.

2 SAMUEL 5:7 NKJV

When David spied out Jerusalem in 1000 BC, it was a forbidding fortress inhabited by an old enemy who declared, "You'll never get in here . . . Even the blind and lame could keep you out!" (v. 6 NLT). End of story? No, just the beginning! The walls were high, the enemy daunting and the voices intimidating, "Nevertheless David took the stronghold . . . dwelt in [it] . . . and called it the City of David" (vv. 7-9 NKJV). Now that's what you call turning the tables!

What's your stronghold, the one area where Satan's strong enough to hold you? A sharp tongue? A judgmental attitude? Low self-esteem? A losing battle with a stubborn habit? When the enemy says, "You're stuck, you'll never get out," God says, "Nevertheless [even so . . . despite how it looks on the surface]." Strongholds mean nothing to God; His "mighty weapons . . . knock down the devil's strongholds" (2Co 10:4 TLB). And He will do for you what He did for David once you understand two important principles: (1) There are two voices continually competing for your attention. One says, "You can do it; don't give up!" The other says, "It's hopeless; you'll never make it!" Follow David and practice selective hearing. Tune out the voices that taunt you from your stronghold. Instead of dialoging with the Devil, say what Jesus said: "Get thee behind me, Satan" (Mt 16:23). (2) Look through eyes of faith. Where others saw walls, David saw tunnels; they focused on the problems while he looked for the possibilities. And because he did what nobody expected, he accomplished what nobody envisioned—and with God's help you can too.

GOD'S WORD FOR ME TODAY IS . . .

You can do it; don't give up!

DAY 31

YOU HAVE ACCESS TO GOD

Let's walk right up to him and get what he is so ready to give.

HEBREWS 4:16 TM

If you've been to an amusement park you know that it's designed to transport you to another world. The goal of the entire experience is to help you lose yourself in its joy and excitement. In prayer, we're transported to another world. Now, a theme park is all make-believe; you have to leave it and come back to the real world. But there is no make-believe with prayer. It takes us into the heavenly realm where Jesus is sitting at the right hand of God. It positions us to hear from God. Hear what? Hear God's voice applying His Word to our specific needs and circumstances. But let's admit it, prayer can be hard work; it requires discipline. It's not as easy as running around having fun at an amusement park. All of us know what it's like to get down on our knees with the best of intentions, and either fall asleep, run out of things to say, or find our minds wandering after just a few minutes.

"Prayer changes things," as the old saying goes, but it first has to change us: to turn us from a self-focus to a God-focus so we can understand and do His will. The writer to the Hebrews puts it this way: "We don't have a priest who is out of touch with our reality. He's been through weakness and testing, experienced it all—all but the sin. So let's walk right up to him and get what he is so ready to give. Take the mercy, accept the help" (vv. 14-16 TM). Today you have access to God through prayer. Use it!

GOD'S WORD FOR ME TODAY IS . . .

Prayer takes us into the heavenly realm where Jesus is sitting at the right hand of God.

DAY 32

STOP WORRYING!

It begins and ends with faith . . . those who are right with God . . . live by faith.

ROMANS 1:17 NCV

A man who maintained he'd swallowed a horse was referred to a psychiatrist, who recommended surgery. The surgeon agreed to bring a horse into the operating room so that when the man woke up he'd know the operation was a success. But after regaining consciousness the man opened his eyes and announced, "That's the wrong horse. It's white. The one I swallowed was black!" Too much anxiety and not enough reality—it's why Christ talks to us so much about worry (which means to be divided or distracted). Understand this. Worry:

(a) Wastes your time and energy. Jesus said, "Who of you by worrying can add a single hour to his life?" (Mt 6:27 NIV). It's a medically proven fact that worry won't lengthen or enrich your life, but it can shorten it. (b) Stops you from enjoying what you have. How? By creating burdens God never intended you to carry—because they're His. (c) Makes you feel less-than. Jesus pointed out that you're worth much more than the birds of the air, and they don't worry or die from hunger; they simply enjoy life. Come on, if God takes care of them, don't you think He'll take care of you too? (d) Makes you overlook God's promises. "If God didn't hesitate to put everything on the line . . . by sending his . . . Son, is there anything else he wouldn't . . . do for us?" (Ro 8:32 TM). Note the word "anything." That covers whatever you're going through right now, plus whatever comes up in the future. So stop worrying.

GOD'S WORD FOR ME TODAY IS . . .

You're worth much more than the birds of the air, and they don't worry or die from hunger; they simply enjoy life.

DAY 33

DEPEND ON GOD

Jacob was left alone.

GENESIS 32:24

Like Jacob, many of us know how it feels to be "left alone." When a loved one dies or a friend leaves, or you walk through the fire of separation and divorce, no matter how "spiritual" you are it still hurts! Emotional pain is to the soul what physical pain is to the body; it tells you something's wrong, that you need God to guide you through the challenges and upheavals of realigning your life to cope with what has happened. And the struggle doesn't begin in earnest while you're surrounded by people, it starts when you've been left alone. The fact is you can survive without others, but you can't survive without God. That's why He sometimes strips away everything that makes us dependent on people. He sends certain individuals into your life to help build your faith and develop your character, and when they're gone, to leave you with the assurance that God's in control. The loss of loved ones: (a) develops our spiritual muscle; (b) tests our resilience; (c) shows us the scope of God's power. When Moses died and Joshua was left in charge, God told him, "As I was with Moses, so I will be with thee" (Jos 1:5). That's something Joshua could never have learned while Moses was in the picture. And it's a lesson you can't learn while you're looking to other human beings for all your answers.

In Mark 4:39 when Jesus "ordered the wind and waves to be quiet" the Bible says "everything was calm" (CEV). In the midst of the storm, ask Him to come and stand in the bow of your boat, and to speak peace to the thing that's upsetting you. He'll do it!

GOD'S WORD FOR ME TODAY IS . . .

You can survive without others, but you can't survive without God.

DAY 34

COMFORT IN TROUBLED TIMES

God will help her at break of day.

PSALM 46:5 NIV

When your world is suddenly turned upside down, remember, God's plans for your life haven't been canceled! When you feel trapped with no way out, here are some things to remember:

(1) Look for the river. "There is a river whose streams make glad" (v. 4 NIV). In Old Testament symbolism, rivers represent God's supply for your every need. When every human source of supply seems to have dried up, don't fear, look for the river. (2) Look for the city. God has planted His "city . . . the holy place where the Most High dwells" (v.4 NIV), right in the middle of your circumstances. God's city, the symbol of His presence and power, guarantees He's still in control and that He will restore peace and order to your troubled world. (3) Look for the signs of God's presence. "God will help [you] at break of day" (v.5 NIV). Daybreak, a symbol of new beginnings, gives you confidence that beyond this time of trouble and testing, a new day is at hand. "Great is his faithfulness; his mercies begin afresh each morning" (La 3:23 NLT). (4) Look at God's track record. "Come . . . see the works of the Lord" (Ps 46:8 NIV). Reviewing the record of His mighty acts builds your faith and reminds you that He is the "same yesterday and today and forever" (Heb 13:8 NIV). If He took care of you then, He will take care of you now. (5) Look to God and be at peace. Based on the tested and proven foundation of His power and faithfulness, you can live by the Scripture: "Be still, and know that I am God" (Ps 46:10 NIV).

GOD'S WORD FOR ME TODAY IS . . .

God's plans for your life haven't been cancelled.

DAY 35

GET TO KNOW GOD BETTER

Can you discover the depths of God?

JOB 11:7 NAS

You're on the adventure of a lifetime when you pursue a greater knowledge of God. What you've learned about God so far should give you a hunger to know Him even more. You must never be satisfied with what you know about Him already. Here are four practical benefits of knowing God:

(1) Blessing. The more you know God and obey His will, the more you'll experience His blessing. "If you obey all the decrees and commands I am giving you today, all will be well with you and your children" (Dt 4:40 NLT). (2) Peace. "Grace and peace be multiplied to you in the knowledge of God" (2Pe 1:2 NAS). The more you know God, the more at peace you'll be. Yes, struggles and setbacks will come, but even then you'll have a sense of wellbeing because you'll feel His nearness. (3) Wisdom. Paul prayed that God would give the Ephesians "a spirit of wisdom and of revelation in the knowledge of Him" (Eph 1:17 NAS). Wisdom is seeing things the right way. Revelation is when God bypasses the limitations of your mind and shows you things you otherwise wouldn't know. Instead of finding a solution to life's problems every now and then, you can walk each day in a "spirit of wisdom and of revelation." (4) Freedom. "When you did not know God, you were slaves to those which by nature are no gods" (Gal 4:8 NAS). Without the confidence that comes from knowing God, and your standing before Him, you become a slave to circumstances, emotions, or other people's opinions. Refuse to live that way. Instead, get to know God better.

GOD'S WORD FOR ME TODAY IS . . .

The more you know God and obey His will, the more you'll experience His blessing.

DAY 36

THINKING OF QUITTING? DON'T!

Be steadfast.

1 CORINTHIANS 15:58 NKJV

George Frideric Handel was a musical prodigy. At twenty-one he was a keyboard virtuoso. When he turned to composing he gained immediate fame and soon was appointed Kapellmeister to the Elector of Hanover (later King George I of England). When Handel moved to England his renown grew. By the time he was forty he was world famous. But despite his talent and fame he faced considerable adversity. Rivalry with English composers was fierce. Audiences were fickle; sometimes they didn't turn out for his performances. He was the victim of the changing political winds. Several times he found himself on the verge of bankruptcy. His problems were compounded by failing health. He suffered a stroke which left his right arm limp and damaged the use of four fingers in his right hand. Although he recovered, it left him battling depression. Finally, at fifty-six, Handel decided it was time to retire. Discouraged, miserable and consumed with debt, he felt certain he'd land in a debtor's prison. So on April 8, 1741, he gave what he considered his farewell concert. Disappointed and filled with self-pity, he gave up. But that year something incredible happened. A wealthy friend named Charles Jennings encouraged Handel by visiting him and giving him a libretto based on the life of Christ. The work intrigued Handel so he began writing. Immediately the floodgates of inspiration opened. For three weeks he wrote almost nonstop. Then he spent another two days creating the orchestrations. In twenty-four days he had completed the 260-page manuscript of Messiah. Thinking of quitting? Don't! "Be steadfast."

GOD'S WORD FOR ME TODAY IS . . .

Don't quit!

DAY 37

LIVING BY "THE FAITH RULE"

These all died in faith.

HEBREWS 11:13 NKJV

The Bible says, "These all died in faith, not having received the promises, but having seen them afar off were assured of them." People of faith anticipate what God promised, whether they ever experience its fulfillment or not. "How can I believe in a promise I don't see fulfilled?" you ask. People like Abraham didn't live to see the ultimate fulfillment of God's promise in their lives, yet they died believing it. Trusting God means banking on His Word, even when there's nothing visible to demonstrate that what He says is going to come true. Even when you're on your deathbed and it still hasn't happened, you still trust Him. That's living by faith. The words "in faith" in this Scripture are different from the words used in all the verses that read "by faith." The words "in faith" actually mean "according to faith." These people lived by "the faith rule." Faith was the ruling principle in their lives! So even if they went to their graves without seeing God's promises fulfilled, they exited saying, "God still told the truth." They knew that the fulfillment was coming, and they lived in anticipation of it. That's what God is asking of you today. He wants you to live before Him in such a way that you anticipate His promises, even when every circumstance seems opposite to what those promises say. It also means you don't manipulate the circumstances to "help God out" as Sarah did when she produced Ishmael. It means trusting God to do it His way, in His time, and for His glory.

GOD'S WORD FOR ME TODAY IS . . .

Trusting God means banking on His Word, even when there's nothing visible to demonstrate that what He says is going to come true.

DAY 38

RECOVERING FROM LOSS

Pour out your heart before Him.

PSALM 62:8 NKJV

Here are five keys to recovering from loss:

(1) Process your grief. Emotions like fear, anger, worry, depression, resentment, helplessness and grief are normal. It's no good to stuff them or deny they exist. God created us to feel; He doesn't expect us to act happy when we're grieving. "Blessed are those who mourn, for they will be comforted" (Mt 5:4 NIV). Be honest with God. "Pour out your heart before Him," and He will comfort you. (2) Accept help. It's a mistake to isolate yourself in the aftermath of a tragedy. We all need the encouragement and the support of others. We're called to carry one another's burdens (See Gal 6:2). (3) Choose the right response. When you choose bitterness, you hurt yourself and shut the door on happiness because you can't be happy and bitter at the same time. During some recent California wildfires there were victims who said, "We've lost everything and we're sad, but we'll work together as a family and rebuild." Others said, "My life's over! I can't go on . . . I'll never recover." You can choose to believe you're on your own, or that God's with you and bounce back. (4) Know your joy comes from God. There's no correlation between your circumstances and your joy. Joy comes from within; it's based on whom you trust, not what you see and feel. (5) Concentrate on what you've got, not on what you've lost. Make a list of the good things in your life, and thank God for what you still have. It's impossible to be grateful and hopeless at the same time.

GOD'S WORD FOR ME TODAY IS . . .

There's no correlation between your circumstances and your joy.

DAY 39

THE ULTIMATE GUARANTEE

Having believed, you were marked . . . with a seal.

EPHESIANS 1:13 NIV

Jesus said, "I give them eternal life, and they shall never lose it" (Jn 10:28 AMP). As parents we understand this. When our children fall we pick them up. We correct them, but we don't disown them. They were born with our DNA and will die with it. And God has the same relationship with us. When we believe and become "children of God" He alters our lineage, redefines our spiritual parenthood, and in doing so secures our salvation. To accomplish this, He seals us with His Spirit. "Having believed, you were marked . . . with a seal, the promised Holy Spirit."

Max Lucado writes: "For a short time in college I worked in a vacuum-cleaner plant. We assembled the appliance from plug to hose. The last step on the assembly line was 'sealing and shipping.' By this point the company had invested hours and dollars in the machine. So they took extra care to protect it. They mummified it in bubble wrap, secured it with Styrofoam, wrapped the box with tough-to-tear tape, stamped the destination on the box, and belted it inside the truck. That machine was secure. But compared to God's care for His saints, the machine [might as well have been] dumped into the back of a pick-up truck. God vacuum-seals us with His strongest force: His Spirit. He sheathes His children in a suit of spiritual armor, encircles us with angels, and indwells us Himself. The Queen of England should enjoy such security." Good news: God has "identified you as his own, guaranteeing that you will be saved on the day of redemption" (Eph 4:30 NLT).

GOD'S WORD FOR ME TODAY IS . . .

God sheathes His children in a suit of spiritual armor, encircles us with angels, and indwells us Himself.

DAY 40

"COME AND SEE"

They came and saw . . . and remained with Him.

JOHN 1:39 NKJV

For John and Andrew, it wasn't enough to listen to John the Baptist. Most of us would have been content to be around the nation's most famous evangelist. Could there be a better teacher? Yes. And when John and Andrew met Jesus, the One John the Baptist spoke about, they left John and followed Him. Notice the request they made: "Where are You staying?" (v. 38 NKJV). Jesus replied, "'Come and see.' They came and saw . . . and remained with Him" (v.39 NKJV). They wanted to know Jesus; to find out what caused His head to turn and His heart to burn and His soul to yearn; to look in His face and follow in His steps. They wanted to know if He could be who John said He was—and if He was, what on earth was He doing? And you can't answer such a question by talking to others, you've got to spend time with "The Man" Himself. Jesus' answer to the disciples, and to you, is, "Come and see." See what?

(1) See how He handles power. Not once did Jesus use His power to impress others or enrich Himself in any way. (2) See how He handles people. He didn't see them as interruptions, irritations or obstacles on His path to personal fulfillment. No. "When He saw the multitudes, He was moved with compassion" (Mt 9:36 NKJV). (3) See how He handles priorities. "Vast crowds came to hear him . . . But Jesus often withdrew to the wilderness for prayer" (Lk 5:15-16 NLT). Did He know something we don't? No commitment is harder to keep, or more important, than spending time in prayer each day.

GOD'S WORD FOR ME TODAY IS . . .

You've got to spend time with "The Man" Himself, Jesus!

DAY 41

"JOSEPH PRINCIPLES"

God has made me forget.

GENESIS 41:51 NKJV

Joseph was thirty when he became governor of Egypt. He was seventeen when he was sold into slavery. For thirteen years he dealt with pain and confusion, maintained his character and his commitment to God, and allowed his trials to make him triumphant. So you can't just throw in the towel, have a pity party, or sit around doing nothing.

Joseph didn't simply forget what happened. Anybody who tells you, "Just forget it," isn't living in the real world. It happened, but God can use it to enrich your life. God gave Joseph two sons: he named them Manasseh, which means "God has made me forget," and Ephraim, which means "God made me fruitful in the land of my afflictions." God gave Joseph new relationships to replace the old ones. One reason why old relationships may be destroying you is that you haven't replaced them with new ones. You're hanging out with the wrong reminders. God helped Joseph to forget the pain of what happened. He still had the memory, but he prospered in spite of it. When you walk with God, the promise before you is always greater than the pain behind you. But here are some "Joseph principles" you need to live by: (1) Don't try to ignore or pretend it never happened. God will give you the grace to handle it, not deny it. (2) Believe that God can "make up to you" the time, the relationships and the opportunities you've lost (See Joel 2:25). (3) List the people who've wronged you, forgive them and release them to God in prayer (See Col 3:13 NLT). (4) Tell God you're ready to start over. And start today!

GOD'S WORD FOR ME TODAY IS . . .

When you walk with God, the promise before you is always greater than the pain behind you.

DAY 42

YOUR MOUNTAIN IS A MOLEHILL

Who are you, O great mountain?

ZECHARIAH 4:7 NKJV

When the Israelites were building the temple, their enemies became like a mountain standing in their way. If that's your situation today, read these words carefully: "This is the word of the Lord to Zerubbabel: 'Not by might nor by power, but by My Spirit,' says the Lord of hosts. 'Who are you, O great mountain? Before Zerubbabel you shall become a plain! And he shall bring forth the capstone with shouts of 'Grace, grace to it!' . . . 'The hands of Zerubbabel have laid the foundation of this temple; his hands shall also finish it . . . For who has despised the day of small things?'" (vv. 6-10 NKJV). The Amplified Bible reads, "O great mountain . . . you shall become a plain [a mere molehill]!" Start looking at your situation from the perspective of God's enabling grace. In this passage the Lord tells Zechariah that the problem facing the Israelites only appeared to be a mountain; it was actually a molehill. How would you like your mountain to become a molehill? It will, once you start doing what God says. Instead of obsessing over the problem, focus on the Lord and His power.

In the early stages of anything you should live by the words, "Don't despise the day of small things." In the middle stages you must live by the words, "Let us not grow weary while doing good" (Gal 6:9 NKJV). And in the final stages, "Looking unto Jesus, the author and finisher of our faith" (Heb 12:2 NKJV). If God's told you to do something, it is not only His will that you begin it, but that you finish it.

GOD'S WORD FOR ME TODAY IS . . .

Instead of obsessing over the problem,
focus on the Lord and His power.

DAY 43

JUST DO IT!

A doubtful mind will be as unsettled as a wave.

JAMES 1:6 TLB

The Bible says: "A doubtful mind will be as unsettled as a wave . . . driven and tossed by the wind. People like that should not expect to receive anything from the Lord. They can't make up their minds" (See Jas 1:6-8 TLB). This Scripture applies specifically to asking God for wisdom, then rationalizing and vacillating when He gives you an answer. But the same principle applies to all of life. Have you ever seen anything more fickle than a wave? The wind that takes it one direction today, takes it in an entirely different one tomorrow. "How does this apply to me?" you ask: (1) If you've grown up in a family where every decision was made for you. (2) If you've spent your life around people who made reckless decisions that left you feeling "it's too easy to get it wrong and too hard to get it right." (3) If the bad decisions you've made in the past have sabotaged your confidence—then today's devotion is just for you!

James makes the point that none of us learn to hear from God without making mistakes. So don't be hard on yourself. Learn from your mistakes, correct the ones you can, and continue being decisive. Don't fall back into a pattern of indecision because you got it wrong a few times. Often you'll only know that you've done the right thing—when you do it! Devote a reasonable amount of time to waiting on God, and when necessary seek the counsel of others. But don't be afraid to act; make a decision and follow through with it. In other words, "Just do it!"

GOD'S WORD FOR ME TODAY IS . . .

Learn from your mistakes, correct the ones you can, and continue being decisive.

DAY 44

HOW TO HAVE A GOOD DAY

Without Me you can do nothing.

JOHN 15:5 NKJV

When Satan has negative plans for your day—you can change the course of your day by spending time with the Lord, especially when you sense any attitude or behavior in yourself that's not Christ-like. Jesus said, "Without Me you can do nothing." On the other hand, through Him we can do all things (See Php 4:13). Negative feelings are like unwelcome house guests: the worst thing you can do is to invite them in. You may not be able to override them in your own strength, but if you seek God's help He will enable you to walk according to His ways, not by your negative emotions and perspective. "But what if someone offends me?" The Bible says we're not to be oversensitive or easily offended. Actually we are commanded to forgive those who hurt us, not let things fester. Sometimes we want to forgive and do what's right, but we find doing it difficult. More often than not, the right thing is the hard thing to do, not the easy thing. That's when you need to pray and allow God to talk to you through His Word. Only then will you find the strength to do the right thing.

Remember, you're in a war, and the battle begins the moment your eyes open each morning. To win, you must know how to use the weapons God has placed at your disposal. And you must put on your armor before the battle begins (See Eph 6:10-20). Your greatest weapons are prayer, praise, reading God's Word, and Christian fellowship. If you want to have a good day, learn to use them.

GOD'S WORD FOR ME TODAY IS . . .

Negative feelings are like unwelcome house guests; the worst thing you can do is invite them in.

DAY 45

HOW TO OVERCOME IN TROUBLED TIMES

Let not your heart be troubled.

JOHN 14:27 NKJV

Jesus said, "My peace I give to you . . . Let not your heart be troubled, neither let it be afraid." Underline the words, "Let not." You can't control what goes on around you, but Jesus said you can control what goes on inside you. How? By doing two things:

(1) Fill your mind with God's Word. Jesus said, "These things I have spoken to you, that in Me you may have peace. In the world you will have tribulation; but be of good cheer, I have overcome the world" (Jn 16:33 NKJV). Rearrange your priorities and take time to read God's Word each day. Process it, apply it to each circumstance, and stand on it in times of difficulty. You'll be amazed at the results!

(2) Pray about the situation, then leave it confidently in God's hands. Here's a prayer to help you do that: "Lord, everything seems to be falling apart around me. Everybody wants a piece of me. There's far too much to do and never enough time to do it. My head is clogged with all kinds of junk and my heart is ready to break. Lord, where are You? I feel like the disciples in the storm, the waves are too big for me. My cry is the same as theirs, 'Somebody go and get Jesus—I'm about to drown out here!' Prince of Peace, I need you. Father, who never slumbers nor sleeps, take charge. Let me find in You a quiet place, a place where I can pillow my head on Your breast, hear Your loving heartbeat and feel secure knowing You'll work things out for me. This I pray, believing, in Jesus' name, amen."

GOD'S WORD FOR ME TODAY IS . . .

You can't control what goes on around you, but Jesus said you can control what goes on inside you.

DAY 46

MAKING THE TOUGH CALLS

The Lord is on my side; I will not fear.

PSALM 118:6 NKJV

All the heroes of the Bible were flawed. And dispositionally, they were as different as chalk and cheese. But they'd one thing in common: they were willing to make the tough calls. Observe: (1) Tough calls demand risk. When the Soviet Union overran and annexed Latvia in 1940, the U.S. Vice Consul in Riga was concerned that the American Red Cross supplies in that city would be looted. To guard against it he requested permission from the State Department in Washington, D.C. to place an American flag above the Red Cross to deter anyone from taking the supplies. "No precedent exists for such action," the Secretary of State's Office cabled back. When the Vice Consul received the message he climbed up and personally nailed the American flag to the pole, then he cabled the State Department: "As of this date, I have established precedent." (2) Tough calls require character. Chuck Swindoll writes: "Courage is not limited to the battlefield or the Indianapolis 500 or bravely catching a thief in your house. The real tests of courage are much quieter. They are the inner tests, like remaining faithful when nobody's looking, like enduring pain when the room is empty, like standing alone when you're misunderstood." Whether you lead a family, a business, or a church, the temptation to complain comes easy. Thank God for the tough times. They're the reason you're there—to be the leader. If everything was going well you wouldn't be needed. When the tough calls must be made, your confidence can be found in these words: "The Lord is on my side; I will not fear."

GOD'S WORD FOR ME TODAY IS . . .

Thank God for the tough times.

DAY 47

GOD WILL TELL YOU WHAT TO SAY

Don't worry about what to say.

MATTHEW 10:19 TLB

Jesus said: "Don't worry about how to respond or what to say. God will give you the right words at the right time. For it is not you who will be speaking—it will be the Spirit of your Father speaking through you" (vv. 19-20 NLT). Does that mean we should not prepare ourselves? No, it just means we should stop trying to figure out in advance everything we need to say and do in every situation we face. You'll wear yourself out trying to prepare for every circumstance you're likely to run into in the future. Jesus told His disciples to entrust their lives fully to God and depend on His indwelling Holy Spirit to guide, protect and equip them when the situation arose. The same goes for us. For example, when we have to make hard decisions or solve complicated problems or confront difficult people, God's Spirit will decide the proper time and the best approach. He will also give us the right words to say. Until then, we don't need to bother ourselves with it. If we will listen to what the Lord is telling us here in this passage, not only will we have more peace, but we will also enjoy more success. When we do have to speak, what comes out of our mouths will be spiritual wisdom from God and not something we have come up with out of our own carnal mind. Your responsibility is not to know the future, it's to trust in God who holds the future, and be confident that you're safe in His hands.

GOD'S WORD FOR ME TODAY IS . . .

God's Spirit will decide the proper time and the best approach.

DAY 48

TAKE A LEAP OF FAITH (1)

You give them something to eat.

MATTHEW 14:16 NKJV

Lee Brown noticed a little girl begging in her neighborhood. Later she searched, but couldn't find her at the local school. That day Brown decided to make a difference for other kids by adopting a first-grade class in one of the city's lowest-performing schools, pledging to pay for any student wanting to attend college. Brown wasn't wealthy. She was a cotton-picker-turned-real estate agent making $45,000 a year and raising two kids—but she honored that pledge. She's personally contributed $10,000 every year, in addition to raising donations from others. Brown's leap of faith rescued students who'd otherwise end up on the streets.

It takes courage to make a difference, especially when you can't see a way to do it. When he was in Africa, David Livingstone received a letter saying, "We want to send helpers. Have you found a good road into your area yet?" Livingstone wrote back, "If they only want to come when there's a good road, don't send them. I want people who'll come when there's no road!" Surrounded by 5,000 hungry people, Jesus told His disciples, "You give them something to eat." It seemed impossible, but when they obeyed they witnessed a miracle. One writer says: "Christ will lead you into seemingly impossible situations . . . don't avoid them. That's where you'll experience God . . . If you attempt only things you know are possible with the resources you possess . . . you'll receive the credit and God will have no part in it . . . Have you received a word that awaits your next step of faith? Proceed, no matter how incredible it seems. You'll experience the joy of seeing God perform a miracle, and so will those around you."

GOD'S WORD FOR ME TODAY IS . . .

It takes courage to make a difference, especially when you can't see a way to do it.

DAY 49

TAKE A LEAP OF FAITH (2)

Faith is . . . the conviction of things not seen.

HEBREWS 11:1 NAS

One day two caterpillars were plodding up a hill when they noticed a butterfly dipping and weaving overhead. Turning to his buddy, one said, "You'd never get me up in one of those things!" Raise your sights, take a leap of faith! "Faith is . . . the conviction of things not seen."

Glynnis Whitwer says: "God calls us to obedience without showing us the end result . . . There are days I'm tired of getting called out of my comfort zone . . . I've been known to whine and ask if I can serve God from the safety of my recliner. But that's not God's way. He doesn't want me limited by my desire for security and control . . . Something inside is revealed when we're pressured from without . . . [it] shines light on the truth about our faith . . . To grow, faith must be stretched, and that's uncomfortable . . . Unlike some, I haven't learned to trust God the easy way . . . by reading a book . . . listening to a sermon . . . or hearing how my friend trusts Him. I'm learning by stepping out into the adventure of obedience and discovering that He's trustworthy. This happened when my husband and I started tithing (after I resisted for years), and watched God cover our needs and more . . . When I obeyed His command to write a book (although I didn't know what I'd write about), and watched God open doors of opportunity . . . When we said yes to adoption, and are watching the blossoming of two little girls with hope and a future . . . Obeying when God hasn't revealed the steps . . . or the final destination is challenging. But when we walk by faith He gets the glory, because we know we couldn't have done it." So, take a leap of faith.

GOD'S WORD FOR ME TODAY IS . . .

When we walk by faith He gets the glory, because we know we couldn't have done it.

DAY 50

BE FAITHFUL TO THE SCRIPTURES

All Scripture is God-breathed.

2 TIMOTHY 3:16 NIV

The first lie ever recorded was the one Satan told Eve when he said that God didn't really mean what He said. And he's still peddling the same line. You hear it in comments like: (a) "If you're sincere, it doesn't matter what you believe." What if you're sincerely wrong? If your car brakes don't work your sincerity won't stop you; telephone poles and buildings will. (b) "We must be careful not to offend anyone." What if people don't want to hear the truth or live according to it? Should we soften or edit the Scriptures based on what we think they can handle? If you love someone, wouldn't you interrupt their sleep to keep them from burning up with the house? (c) "There is truth in the Bible, but not all the Bible is true." Paul writes that "All Scripture is God-breathed." And Isaiah says, "If they speak not according to this word, it is because there is no light in them" (Isa 8:20). Twelve inches must make one foot, otherwise we're all open to each other's interpretations and subject to each other's value judgments—and somebody's going to get the short end of the stick.

Now, when we become arrogant in presenting the truth, the cause of Christ suffers and spiritually hungry people are turned off. We who have received grace and mercy must show it. But let's not compromise what God's Word says. Interestingly, when polled recently, the majority of today's young people (16-29) said, "Give it to me straight. And if you don't live it, don't give it!" How refreshing! Bottom line: God's Word is wholly, solely, fully, completely and altogether true. So be faithful to the Scriptures!

GOD'S WORD FOR ME TODAY IS . . .

We who have received grace and mercy must show it.

DAY 51

IT'S ALL PART OF HIS PLAN

In everything God works for the good of those who love him . . . because that was his plan.

ROMANS 8:28 NCV

When you're in a situation where you've got more questions than answers, it takes faith to accept that "in everything God works for the good of those who love him." What you consider wasted experiences can become confidence-builders and priceless sources of insight—when you make up your mind to learn from them! If you don't, they'll keep happening until you do. The Israelites went in circles for forty years before they finally wised up. Don't let that happen to you.

When you get too comfortable God stirs things up. The mother eagle teaches her little ones to fly by making their nest so uncomfortable that they're forced out of it. Next they are pushed off a cliff edge. Can you imagine their thoughts: "It's my mother doing this?" Who and where you are at this moment in time has been divinely appointed. God in His wisdom knows that you need the challenge of certain situations to mature and stretch you. The job you dread going to every day is developing your skills, endurance and sense of responsibility. Those people who rub you the wrong way are actually making you more like Jesus! Paul says, God "understands . . . and knows what is best for us at all times" (Eph 1:8 TLB). So instead of asking Him to change things, thank Him for the experience and the lessons you're learning. And if you can't figure out what those lessons are, ask Him. James says, "If . . . you need wisdom . . . ask God" (Jas 1:5 CEV). When you do, you'll discover—it's all part of His plan!

GOD'S WORD FOR ME TODAY IS . . .

God in His wisdom knows that you need the challenge of certain situations to mature and stretch you.

DAY 52

KNOWING GOD BETTER

The Spirit will take from what is mine and make it known to you.

JOHN 16:15 NIV

Spiritual activities can never replace spiritual intimacy. A lot of us go to church with the wrong focus. We want to know what the pastor's subject is. What we should be thinking is: "Lord, whatever the preacher says today, I want You to speak to me personally so I'll know what Your will is for my situation." When God's Word starts coming alive for you in ways that change you and take you in a direction you would never have discovered for yourself, you're on the same wavelength as the Holy Spirit, whose job is to clarify and reveal God's purpose for your life. Living on this wavelength puts you in a world apart from others, even many professing Christians.

Paul said in First Corinthians, chapter two, verse fourteen, that the "natural man" (NAS) can't grasp anything from God because his spirit is dead. He says the things of God are "foolishness" to such a person. So a mature believer is worlds removed from the understanding of the spiritually dull or dead person. The truth is, even church-goers don't understand the mature believer. Paul said such a person "is appraised [properly understood and evaluated] by no one" (1Co 2:15 NAS). Folks can't figure mature believers out because they have "the mind of Christ" (v. 16 NIV). This kind of intimacy with God is rare today, even though the mind of Christ is God's will for, and is available to each of us. Spiritually mature believers have a passion to pursue and know God, and they aren't satisfied until they are in an intimate relationship with Him. So make your goal—knowing God better.

GOD'S WORD FOR ME TODAY IS . . .

Spiritual activities can never replace spiritual intimacy.

DAY 53

PRESS THROUGH!

If God is for us, who can be against us?

ROMANS 8:31 NIV

To reach your God-ordained destiny you must do these seven things: (1) Refuse to give in to wrong thoughts. Guard your mind. Make it a walled city that refuses to allow negative thoughts and harmful influences to penetrate. (2) Resist any temptation toward introspection. Only the Holy Spirit has the right to search the hearts and minds of men. When the Lord is ready to reveal an area of your life that needs correction, He will. (3) Fight, using God's Word. Let the Rhema Word, the God-breathed Word found in Scripture, be your strength in times of difficulty and testing. In the wilderness temptation, Jesus used Scripture to put Satan to flight. And the weapon of God's Word still works today. (4) Listen to the still small voice of God within. God doesn't play hide-and-seek with His will. Discipline yourself to spend unhurried time with Him and you'll thrive. (5) Shift to a higher level of faith. Before killing Goliath, David had to kill a lion and a bear. Today we are contending with issues that require us to move to a new level of faith. (6) Get into proper alignment. God's aligning His people—putting together those who'll stand as one in the day of battle. It's imperative to know who you can go to war with. You only discover such people in times of testing. Treasure them; they're "covenant relationships." (7) Ask God to give you understanding about the place you are in. Knowing you are in preparation for your destiny will keep you from pulling back, vacillating or throwing in the sponge. The word for you today is—press through and seize your God-given destiny!

GOD'S WORD FOR ME TODAY IS . . .

Press through and seize your God-given destiny.

DAY 54

A CONSCIENCE—GROUNDED IN GOD'S WORD

Holding on to faith and a good conscience.

1 TIMOTHY 1:19 NIV

Paul writes to Timothy: "My son, I give you this instruction in keeping with the prophecies once made about you, so that by following them you may fight the good fight, holding on to faith and a good conscience. Some have rejected these and so have shipwrecked their faith. Among them are Hymenaeus and Alexander" (vv. 18-20 NIV). What do we know about Hymenaeus and Alexander? Not much. But what we do know is sobering. Having failed to develop, protect, and live by a conscience grounded in God's Word, they ended up spiritually shipwrecked. What a picture. A fine sea-going vessel lies shattered on the rocks because it got off course. The saying, "Let conscience be your guide," needs one more phrase added: "As long as your conscience is grounded in God's Word." When we want to do our own thing and go our own way, we tend to justify it by saying, "If it feels so right how can it be wrong?" Understand this: if God's Word says something is wrong—it's wrong, no matter how right it feels! Your conscience must line up with the unchanging truth of Scripture. When the ultimate arbiter of your choices and actions is "feelings," the winds of temptation, compromise and comfort will sweep you off course and you'll end up shipwrecked. The apostle John gives us an all-important reason for keeping our conscience in good repair: "If we don't feel guilty, we can come to God with bold confidence. And we will receive from him whatever we ask because we obey him and do the things that please him" (1Jn 3:21-22 NLT).

GOD'S WORD FOR ME TODAY IS . . .

Your conscience must line up with the unchanging truth of Scripture.

DAY 55

"GIVE GOD THE REINS"

Trust in the Lord with all your heart and lean not on your own understanding.

PROVERBS 3:5 NIV

Cliff Schimmels says: "When I was young my dad had a team of horses. One day he said to me, 'Son, would you like to drive?' So I took the reins. I was in control. I was driving. But the plodding bothered me, it was too slow. So I clucked the horses along and they began to trot. Then Babe and Blue came up with a better idea. They decided that if they ran we would get home faster. Soon they were running as fast as I've ever seen horses run. As the prairie-dog holes whizzed by I concluded that we were in a dangerous situation, so I tried my best to slow down the runaway team. I tugged on the reins until my hands cramped. I cried and pleaded, but nothing worked. Old Babe and Blue just kept running. I glanced over at my dad and he was just sitting there, watching the world go by. By now I was frantic. My hands were cut from the reins, tears streaming down my face, frozen from the winter cold. Finally in desperation I turned to my dad and said, 'Here, take the reins, I don't want to drive anymore.' Now that I'm older and people call me grandpa, I re-enact that scene at least once a day."

Regardless of how old we get or how capable we think we are, there's always that moment when the only way out is to turn to our heavenly Father and say, "Here, take the reins, I don't want to drive any more." And He will, but you've got to give them to Him!

GOD'S WORD FOR ME TODAY IS . . .

Trust in the Lord with all your heart.

DAY 56

TRUSTING GOD IN THE DARK

You do not realize now what I am doing, but later you will.

JOHN 13:7 NIV

Mary and Martha were upset that Jesus didn't come until their brother Lazarus was dead. "Lord . . . if you had been here, my brother would not have died" (Jn 11:21 & 32 NIV). But instead of giving them reasons, Jesus replied, "Did I not tell you . . . if you believed, you would see [God glorified in this?]" (v. 40 NIV). When God asked Abraham to sacrifice his son Isaac he didn't understand, but later he witnessed God's faithfulness when Isaac was restored to him. Moses didn't understand why he had to spend forty years in the wilderness, but later when God called him to lead Israel to freedom, he got it. Joseph didn't know why his brothers mistreated him or why he was imprisoned unfairly, but later he saw God's hand in everything. His father questioned why Joseph had been taken away from him, but later, looking into the face of the man who had been made governor and who'd saved the lives of the nation, God's purposes became clear.

Just like your children don't always think your decisions make sense, we don't understand God's ways. That's why Jesus said to Mary and Martha, "You do not realize now what I am doing, but later you will." God doesn't expect you to understand, but He does expect you to trust Him. In spite of his boils, bankruptcy and bereavement Job said, "When he has tested me, I will come forth" (Job 23:10 NIV). Is God testing you in this situation? If He is, what are you learning? Is the experience making you bitter, or making you better by causing you to draw closer to Him?

GOD'S WORD FOR ME TODAY IS . . .

God doesn't expect you to understand, but He does expect you to trust Him.

119

DAY 57

SEEING YOUR TRIALS THE RIGHT WAY

Blessed is a man who perseveres under trial.

JAMES 1:12 NAS

Too many of us view our trials the way we watch television. Some televisions have a second channel in the corner of your screen that enables you to divide your focus and watch two programs at once. A lot of us try to superimpose our human viewpoint on the screen of God's will for our lives. God gives us a divine perspective, then we open up a second screen, a human one, and try to figure it all out. Don't waste your trials by trying to fit them into your limited vision and understanding or you'll end up frustrated. It's much better to trust God, rest in His wisdom and take Him at His word.

A spiritual perspective on your trials will keep you from buckling under the weight of them when times are hard. When you begin to look at your trials from God's perspective, your spirit is renewed and you're enabled to press on and receive what God has waiting for you. James writes: "Blessed is a man who perseveres under trial; for once he has been approved, he will receive the crown of life." Now the Crown of Life is not just something you receive in Heaven, you can enjoy it today. And who's it for? Those who "persevere." When God gives you this Crown, He's saying, "You've passed another of life's tests, now you're ready for a new level of blessing." Remember the wonderful feeling you had when you passed some of your hardest tests in school? Don't get discouraged. God is up to something good. Keep going—don't stop until you receive the Crown of Life.

GOD'S WORD FOR ME TODAY IS . . .

Trust God, rest in His wisdom and take Him at His word.

DAY 58

LEARNING TO HEAR GOD'S VOICE

His sheep follow him because they know his voice.

JOHN 10:4 NIV

One evening a friend visiting Peter Lord's home told him he could hear no fewer than eighteen different kinds of crickets in his garden. Peter was amazed—he'd lived there for years and never heard one. The difference was, this man was a professor of entomology and he had learned to distinguish over two hundred different cricket calls with his natural ear. Imagine learning to listen to crickets! Looking back, Peter wrote: "I suddenly understood that a person must want to hear, and learn to hear, and there were many sounds I was not hearing." Think what you've been missing all these years because you haven't wanted or learned to hear the voice of God speaking to you.

God often speaks to us through others. But the very gifts He speaks to us through can weaken our desire to hear from God for ourselves. The children of Israel said to Moses, "We want you to hear from God for us" (See Ex 20:18-19). The problem is, when you only hear from God through secondary sources it's easier not to make any real commitment, or to obey what you've heard. But when you know God is speaking to you personally you must make a clear-cut decision. Jesus said, "His sheep follow him because they know his voice." Examine the "heroes" in your Bible. They were all flawed! So what gave them the strength to accomplish such great things? They knew God's voice! Nothing, absolutely nothing in your life, is more important than learning to know God's voice when He speaks to you!

GOD'S WORD FOR ME TODAY IS . . .

Learn to know God's voice when He speaks to you.

DAY 59

BE PATIENT, IT'LL HAPPEN IN GOD'S TIME!

Rest in the Lord, and wait patiently for him.

PSALM 37:7

The old saying, "You can't always have what you want," isn't necessarily true. When you "Delight yourself in the Lord . . . he will give you the desires of your heart" (v. 4 NIV). But usually He makes you wait. Dennis Wholey says: "Waiting is an art . . . If you can wait two years, you can achieve something you couldn't achieve today however hard you worked, however much money you threw at it, however many times you banged your head against the wall." There are things you can't have today that you'll be able to have in the future. So it doesn't make sense to drive yourself crazy and put your life on hold struggling to accomplish something now, that'll be easy when the time is right.

James says, "Don't try to get out of anything prematurely. Let it do its work so you become mature" (Jas 1:4 TM). God allows certain things to take place in our lives to teach us important principles like: (a) developing new skills and ways of thinking; (b) showing grace and controlling our responses; (c) maintaining our faith when times get tough. Paul writes: "Patience . . . [is . . . the power to endure whatever comes, with good temper]" (Col 3:12 AMP). "Be glad for all God is planning . . . Be patient in trouble, and prayerful always" (Ro 12:12 TLB). When you spend time in God's waiting room, He's developing qualities in you that simply can't be developed any other way. When He's finished you'll come out stronger and wiser. And you'll have the maturity to handle what He has in mind for you. So don't let the Enemy rattle you or engineer circumstances that put you into overdrive. "Rest in the Lord, and wait patiently for him."

GOD'S WORD FOR ME TODAY IS . . .

When He's finished you'll come out stronger and wiser.

DAY 60

WHY DOES IT TAKE SO LONG?

Practice these things. Devote your life to them.

1 TIMOTHY 4:15 GWT

Why does change take so long? Because: (1) We are slow learners. How often have you failed and thought, "Not again! I thought I knew better." The history of Israel illustrates how quickly we forget the lessons God teaches us and revert to old attitudes and patterns of behavior. That's why "We must pay more careful attention, therefore, to what we have heard, so that we do not drift away" (Heb 2:1 NIV). (2) We have a lot to unlearn. We go to a counselor with a problem that took years to develop and say, "Fix me. I've got an hour." Whoa! Your problems didn't develop overnight and they won't disappear overnight. There's no pill, prayer or principle that will instantly undo the damage of many years. It requires the hard work of removal and replacement. The Bible calls this "Taking off the old self, and putting on the new self" (See Eph 4:22-23 NIV). We still have old patterns, practices and predispositions that need to be dealt with. (3) Growth is painful. Every change involves a loss of some kind. We must let go of our old ways in order to experience the new life Christ promised. And we fear these losses, even if our old ways are self-defeating, because, like a pair of worn-out shoes, they are comfortable and familiar. (4) Habits take time to develop. Your character is the sum total of your habits. And there is only one way to develop the habits of Christ-like character: you must practice them over and over! There are no instant habits. That's why Paul urged Timothy to "Practice these things. Devote your life to them."

GOD'S WORD FOR ME TODAY IS . . .

We must let go of our old ways in order to experience the new life Christ promised.

DAY 61

HAVING A STEADFAST PURPOSE!

You will keep in perfect peace him whose mind is steadfast.

ISAIAH 26:3 NIV

Knowing your purpose gives meaning to your life. This is why people try dubious methods like astrology and psychics to discover it. When your life has a steadfast purpose you can bear almost anything. Without it, nothing is bearable. Isaiah complained, "I have labored to no purpose; I have spent my strength in vain and for nothing" (Isa 49:4 NIV). Job lamented, "I give up; I am tired of living. Leave me alone. My life makes no sense" (Job 7:16 GNT). Dr. Bernie Siegel found that he could predict which of his cancer patients were more likely to survive by asking, "Do you want to live to be 100?" Those with a deep sense of purpose who answered "yes" were the ones who survived most often.

Having a steadfast purpose simplifies life. It defines what you do and what you don't do. It becomes the standard you use to evaluate which activities are essential and which aren't. Without purpose you've no real foundation on which to base your decisions, allocate your time and use your resources. You tend to make choices based on circumstances, pressures, and your mood at that moment. When you don't know your purpose you try to do too much, and that causes stress and conflict. It's impossible to do everything people want you to do; you have just enough time to do God's will. If you can't get it all done, you're trying to do more than God intended. A steadfast purpose makes your lifestyle simpler and your schedule saner. And it leads to peace of mind: "You will keep in perfect peace him whose mind is steadfast."

GOD'S WORD FOR ME TODAY IS . . .

*Having a steadfast purpose defines what you **do** and what you **don't** do.*

DAY 62

SEEING YOURSELF AS GOD DOES (1)

We were like grasshoppers in our own sight.

NUMBERS 13:33 NKJV

When Moses sent twelve spies to check out the Promised Land, ten came back saying, "We saw . . . giants . . . and we were like grasshoppers in our own sight." Israel had repeatedly witnessed God's power; why now were they intimidated? It's a perception problem called low self-esteem, and it's how the Enemy prevents you from winning. The Israelites quickly forgot their Red Sea deliverance and instead remembered Egypt where they'd lived as slaves. Be careful. Hard times can make you think you don't deserve to be blessed! Anytime you have something of value, the Enemy will attack you. In the Old Testament we read: "When the Philistines heard . . . David had been anointed king . . . they went up in full force to search for him" (2Sa 5:17 NIV). Until you claim your rightful place in Christ, Satan will tell you that you deserve to be mistreated. So steep yourself in God's Word till it becomes such a part of you that you stop doubting yourself. God made you in His image, redeemed you, indwells you, and that makes you valuable!

A man in the prairie observed an eagle fatally wounded by gunshot. He writes: "With his eyes gleaming . . . he slowly turned his head, giving one last . . . longing look towards the sky. He'd often swept those starry spaces with his wonderful wings . . . the sky was the home of his heart. There he'd displayed his strength a thousand times . . . played with the lightning and raced the wind. Now far from home, the eagle lay dying, because—just once—he forgot and flew too low . . . My soul is that eagle. This isn't its home. It must never lose its skyward look."

GOD'S WORD FOR ME TODAY IS . . .

God made you in His image, redeemed you, indwells you, and that makes you valuable!

DAY 63

SEEING YOURSELF AS GOD DOES (2)

We . . . are being transformed into his likeness.

2 CORINTHIANS 3:18 NIV

A man who was feeling depressed went to see a psychiatrist. After sharing his problems he expected some profound words of wisdom that would make him feel better. "Well," the psychiatrist exclaimed, "I've diagnosed your problem. It's low self-esteem—and it's very common among losers!" When you view yourself negatively you tend to gravitate toward people who talk down to you. But when you know that God loves you and "plans . . . to give you a future and a hope" (Jer 29:11 NLT), your entire outlook changes. With God you can't lose. Even if you stumble and fall He'll help you to get back up, learn from the experience and move on. When you look at yourself you tend to see somebody who makes mistakes and falls short, right? But when you begin to look at yourself in the mirror of God's Word, you see someone "being transformed into his likeness."

Ever gone to a garage sale or an antique show looking for a bargain? To the untrained eye much of the stuff looks like rubbish; it may even have been gathering dust and mildew in somebody's attic. But the experienced eye sees treasure in disguise, items that just need to be cleaned, polished and restored in order to become valuable again. Well, God's the expert with a trained eye. When the Enemy tells you you're worthless, God looks inside you and sees hidden treasure. When you put Him on the throne of your life He'll enable you to overcome your past, resist temptation, break through your self-imposed limitations, and start accepting that in His eyes you have great worth.

GOD'S WORD FOR ME TODAY IS . . .

*In **His** eyes you have great worth.*

DAY 64

KEEP TREADING AND TRUSTING!

Every place that the sole of your foot shall tread upon, that have I given unto you.

JOSHUA 1:3

You'll notice a common thread throughout the Bible. When we really need Him, God shows up and does for us what we can't do. The rest of the time, which is most of the time, He strengthens us and says "keep treading and trusting." There's no magic carpet. To achieve anything worthwhile you have to walk it out in faith, step by challenging step.

The Book of Job has forty-two chapters. In the first forty-one, Job lived through the loss of his health, his wealth and his family. With friends like Job had, he didn't need any enemies. His doubts were relentless. Over and over he questioned God but got only silence for an answer. He persevered through tough days and sleepless nights believing, "When He has tried me, I shall come forth as gold" (Job 23:10 NAS). Notice: (1) It takes fire to produce gold. (2) Only the refiner knows the degree of heat and amount of time required. (3) To rush the process is to produce something of lesser value.

God told Israel that every place the soles of their feet trod, He would give to them. C. V. White says: "The man who succeeds never waits for the crowd. He strikes out for himself. It takes nerve, it takes a lot of grit, but the man who succeeds has both. Nothing important was ever done but the greater number consulted previously doubted the possibility. Success is the accomplishment of that which people think can't be done." Complacency, fatigue, criticism and discouragement are hurdles you must constantly overcome. So, keep "treading and trusting!"

GOD'S WORD FOR ME TODAY IS . . .

The man who succeeds never waits for the crowd.

DAY 65

SURVIVING A SLUMP

The best . . . I can do is escape to Philistine country.

1 SAMUEL 27:1 TM

In a slump you lose your rhythm, feel sluggish and unfocused, and revert to old habits that didn't work then and don't work now. It happened to David. On the run from Saul and leading a makeshift army, he started thinking, "Sooner or later, Saul's going to get me. The best . . . I can do is escape to Philistine country." David knew better! In past crises he "enquired of the Lord," and consulted trusted advisors. This time he was guided by his fears and ended up defecting to enemy territory. And for a while it felt good. Getting wasted, cheating on your mate, filling your mind with porn may seem enjoyable temporarily, but: "There's a way of life that looks harmless . . . look again—it leads straight to hell . . . people appear to be having a good time, but all that . . . will end in heartbreak" (Pr 14:12-13 TM). Eventually even the Philistines rejected David and said, "He's not going into battle with us. He'd switch sides in the middle of the fight!" (1 Sa 29:4 TM). Be careful; the decisions you make when you're down can have long-lasting ramifications. Rejected by the Philistines, overrun by the Amalekites, with no country of his own and no family to come home to, we learn from David to: (1) Seek wise counselors. It's the last thing you'll feel like doing because misery loves company. But when you "Refuse good advice . . . your plans fail" (Pr 15:22 TM). In fact, "The more wise counsel you follow, the better" (Pr 11:14 TM). (2) Stop listening to your fears and listen to God. Standing among the ruins of his life, "David found strength in the Lord" (1 Sa 30:6 NIV), and you will too.

GOD'S WORD FOR ME TODAY IS . . .

The decisions you make when you're down can have long-lasting ramifications.

DAY 66

DEALING WITH STRONG HOLDS, IMAGINATIONS, AND THOUGHTS

Pulling down . . . strong holds; Casting down imaginations . . . bringing into captivity every thought.

2 CORINTHIANS 10:4-5

Paul writes: "Pulling down . . . strong holds; Casting down imaginations . . . bringing into captivity every thought to the obedience of Christ." What are you to pull down? Strong holds: areas of your life that are held in the grip of the enemy. What are you to cast down? Imaginations: always fearing the worst instead of believing God for the best. What are you to take captive? Thoughts: thinking that doesn't line up with God's Word or submit to the rule of Christ in your life.

Recognize that you are in a war. Old issues and thought patterns will constantly try to reestablish control over you. Don't let them. And be careful who your friends are. If they can barely stay afloat themselves, how can they lift you? So long as these old issues reign in your life, Christ's seat is taken. If they are on the throne, Christ is still on the cross. Put Christ on the throne and your past on the cross!

In the Old Testament a priest could not come into God's presence if he had touched anything dead (See Lev 22:3-4). That means if you are going to walk with God you must bury your old lifestyle. Don't even "touch" those old dead issues any more. It also means forgiving those who hurt you, including yourself, then moving on. The issue is not whether you remember but how you remember. God is able to take the sting out of the memory and still leave the sweet taste of victory intact. No longer will you be handicapped or hindered by what you've been through; instead you'll be enriched by it!

GOD'S WORD FOR ME TODAY IS . . .

Put Christ on the throne and your past on the cross.

DAY 67

THE VERSE AT THE CENTER OF THE BIBLE

It is better to trust in the Lord than to put confidence in man.

PSALM 118:8

Psalm 117 is the shortest chapter in the Bible. Psalm 119 is the longest. Psalm 118 is at the center of the Bible. There are 594 chapters in the Bible before Psalm 118, and 594 chapters after Psalm 118—1,188 chapters. This number can be split 118-8, or Psalm 118:8. Now we know that the chapter divisions in the Bible are not part of original Scripture, but isn't it interesting how this little word-exercise worked out? Or was God in the center of it all? And if He was, shouldn't the central verse of the Bible contain its central theme? It does: "It is better to trust in the Lord than to put confidence in man."

In Psalm 118 the Psalmist recalls seven reasons why God is worthy to be trusted: (a) "I called upon the Lord in distress: the Lord answered me, and set me in a large place" (v. 5). (b) "The Lord is on my side; I will not fear: what can man do unto me?" (v. 6). (c) "The Lord taketh my part with them that help me: therefore shall I see my desire upon them that hate me" (v. 7). (d) "I shall not die, but live, and declare the works of the Lord" (v. 17). (e) "The Lord hath chastened me sore: but he hath not given me over unto death" (v. 18). (f) "This is the day which the Lord hath made; we will rejoice and be glad in it" (v. 24). (g) "Oh, give thanks to the Lord, for He is good! For His mercy endures forever" (v. 29 NKJV).

GOD'S WORD FOR ME TODAY IS . . .

God is worthy to be trusted.

DAY 68

YOU'LL GET THROUGH THIS STORM

It is I; do not be afraid.

MARK 6:50 NKJV

Are you in a storm today? Then read these words: "The boat was in the middle of the sea; and He was alone on the land. Then He saw them straining at rowing, for the wind was against them. Now about the fourth watch of the night He came to them, walking on the sea, and would have passed them by. And when they saw Him walking on the sea, they supposed it was a ghost, and cried out . . . But immediately He talked with them and said to them . . . 'It is I; do not be afraid.' Then He went up into the boat to them, and the wind ceased" (Mk 6:47-51 NKJV). There are four lessons here for us:

(1) It's when we feel most separated from God that He's teaching us the most. Dave Dravecky said: "Looking back . . . I have learned that the wilderness is part of the landscape of faith, and every bit as essential as the mountaintop. On the mountaintop we are overwhelmed by God's presence. In the wilderness we are overwhelmed by His absence. Both places should bring us to our knees; the one, in utter awe; the other, in utter dependence." (2) God doesn't show up early. Usually He comes in the worst part of the storm when you think you can't take any more—but He will always be on time. (3) God takes us through different storms, revealing more of Himself to us in each one. Otherwise, there are aspects of His character and divine strategies we'd never understand. (4) God's presence alone should be enough for us in any storm. That moment when God shows up and says, "It is I," should calm our every fear.

GOD'S WORD FOR ME TODAY IS . . .

God's presence alone should be enough for us in any storm.

DAY 69

HOW TO DEFEAT YOUR GIANT

The battle is the Lord's.

1 SAMUEL 17:47 NKJV

One day a soldier charged with fleeing from the enemy was brought before Alexander the Great. Alexander the Great asked him, "What's your name?" Dropping his head, he replied, "Alexander." Alexander the Great grabbed him by the shoulders and said, "Soldier, change your conduct or change your name!" You have been called to live a life worthy of the One whose name you carry. Regardless of whether the giant you face is addiction, resentment, fear, lust, pride, envy or anger, you must realize:

(1) You're not unique. Your temptations "are no different from what others experience" (1Co 10:13 NLT). Goliath wasn't always a giant; he was fed and nurtured until he became one. Our giants are usually little sins we overlook and indulge until they assume a life of their own and come back to haunt us. (2) You can't do it alone. Your giant will defeat you anytime you tackle him in your own strength. David told Goliath, "This is the Lord's battle, and he will give you to us" (1Sa 17:47 NLT). You need divine help to overcome old habits and establish new behaviors. So, declare with Paul, "Christ . . . gives me strength" (Php 4:13 NLT). (3) You must confront your giant head-on. The Bible says, "As Goliath moved closer to attack, David quickly ran . . . to meet him" (1Sa 17:48 NLT). Don't run away, don't try to negotiate, don't compromise and don't excuse. Force your giant out into the light and don't let him back into your life. Establish boundaries and make yourself accountable. Stay out of the wrong company. Above all, don't look at God in the light of your giant, look at your giant in the light of God.

GOD'S WORD FOR ME TODAY IS . . .

You must confront your giant head-on.

DAY 70

"IT IS WELL WITH MY SOUL"

My peace I give you . . . Do not let your hearts be troubled and . . . afraid.

JOHN 14:27 NIV

The peace Jesus gives brings a sense of assurance that no matter what happens, you know "it is well with my soul." He says to us: "My peace I give you. I do not give to you as the world gives. Do not let your hearts be troubled and . . . afraid." The peace Jesus gives doesn't depend on conditions and circumstances. It comes from knowing you're God's child and that your Father controls the universe, loves you and always has your best interests at heart. That's why people who've lost everything will often tell you they wouldn't trade what they've learned, even if it meant recouping all their losses. Joni Eareckson Tada discovered a supernatural peace when an accident confined her to a wheelchair, and Corrie ten Boom found it in a Nazi death camp. Missionary Elisabeth Elliot found it in ministering to the Indian tribe who massacred her husband. She wrote: "Only in acceptance lies peace . . . not in resignation." There's a big difference! Author Creath Davis points out that: "Resignation is surrender to fate. Acceptance is surrender to God. Resignation lies down quietly in an empty universe. Acceptance rises up to meet the God who fills that universe with purpose and destiny. Resignation says, 'I can't.' Acceptance says, 'God can.' Resignation paralyzes the life process. Acceptance releases the process for its greatest creativity. Resignation says, 'It's all over for me.' Acceptance says, 'Now that I'm here, what's next, Lord?' Resignation says, 'What a waste.' Acceptance says, 'In what redemptive way will you use this mess, Lord?' Resignation says, 'I'm alone.' Acceptance says, 'I belong to you, Lord.'"

GOD'S WORD FOR ME TODAY IS . . .

The peace Jesus gives doesn't depend on conditions and circumstances.

DAY 71

STAYING POWER!

Keep your mind on Jesus [and] . . . you won't get discouraged and give up.

HEBREWS 12:3 CEV

It's difficult to endure hardship at the best of times, but when you don't know why, it can be frustrating. God doesn't give us lengthy explanations on how He works; He's used to creating worlds with a single sentence. So when you don't find an immediate answer in His Word or through prayer or the counsel of others, you're left wondering. And you wouldn't be the first. David repeatedly asks why in the Psalms, and God still called him "a man after My own heart, who will do all My will" (Ac 13:22 NKJV). So don't get discouraged. Bible commentator William Barclay pointed out that endurance isn't just the ability to bear a hard thing, but to use it for your growth and God's glory.

When the answers aren't forthcoming the question then becomes, "How do I get through this?" And the Bible addresses it by telling us Jesus endured "the shame of being nailed to a cross, because he knew . . . later on he would be glad" (Heb 12:2 CEV). Then it goes on to say: "Keep your mind on Jesus . . . you won't get discouraged and give up." The reason Jesus endured was because He was able to look ahead and envision the joy of pleasing His Father, building the church and saving a lost world. The Psalmist said, "I have set the Lord always before me . . . he is at my right hand, I shall not be moved" [discouraged, or thrown by the situation] (Ps 16:8). Staying-power is not denying reality, or white-knuckling it. It's keeping your eyes on Jesus and drawing from Him the strength you need to fight your way through to victory!

GOD'S WORD FOR ME TODAY IS . . .

Staying-power is not denying reality, it's keeping your eyes on Jesus.

DAY 72

BUILD UP YOUR FAITH!

Taking the shield of faith.

EPHESIANS 6:16 NKJV

A Roman soldier's shield protected him from head to toe. It was made of iron, upholstered in thick layers of fabric, and saturated in water when going to battle. Consequently the flaming arrows of the enemy fizzled on contact. Getting the idea? Paul writes: "Take up the shield of faith, with which you can extinguish all the flaming arrows of the evil one" (NIV). Satan can't penetrate a heart that's pure, saturated in Scripture and fortified by faith. That's why Jesus told Peter, "I have prayed for you, that your faith should not fail" (Lk 22:32 NKJV). It's your faith that's under attack; it's your faith that needs to be fed and nurtured; it's your faith that sustains you in life's battles! Jesus said, "Have faith in God" (Mk 11:22). Note, He didn't just say, "Have faith in something bigger than yourself." No, He said, "Have faith in God."

If you're under attack today claim this promise: "He gives power to the weak, and to those who have no might He increases strength. Even the youths shall faint and be weary, and the young men shall utterly fall, but those who wait on the Lord shall renew their strength; they shall mount up with wings like eagles, they shall run and not be weary, they shall walk and not faint" (Isa 40:29-31 NKJV). God gives each of us a "measure of faith" (Ro 12:3 NKJV). But Jude says you must develop it by "building yourselves up on your most holy faith" (Jude v. 20 NKJV). Faith under attack is faith under construction. It's in the battles of life that you discover whether you have nurtured faith or neglected faith!

GOD'S WORD FOR ME TODAY IS . . .

Faith under attack is faith under construction.

DAY 73

LET'S KEEP THE FAITH

Contend earnestly for the faith.

JUDE V. 3 NKJV

The Bible says: "We must give the more earnest heed to the things we have heard, lest we drift away" (Heb 2:1 NKJV). The word "drift" should set off alarm bells. Jesus pointed out that while the harvesters slept an enemy sowed weeds among the wheat. When they finally wakened they said, "An enemy has done this" (Mt 13:28 NKJV). Cancer begins with one unidentified, unchecked cell, and if left un-dealt-with it can destroy your whole body. Hence Jude writes: "Contend earnestly for the faith which was once for all delivered to the saints. For certain men have crept in unnoticed, who long ago were marked out for this condemnation, ungodly men, who turn the grace of our God into lewdness and deny the only Lord God and our Lord Jesus Christ" (vv. 3-4 NKJV). Note the words "the faith which was once for all delivered to the saints." Our methods may change, but our message never changes. Paul writes: "The time will come when they will not endure sound doctrine" (2Ti 4:3 NKJV). Study the progression in the lives of Abraham, Isaac and Jacob. Abraham's blessings came through a personal relationship with God. Isaac inherited his father's blessings. Not until the Philistines attacked him, did he go back and dig again the wells of his father Abraham and build an altar to the Lord. Finally Jacob, the third generation, came along and tried schemes and shortcuts to obtain God's blessing. Only when he had a life-changing encounter with God at Peniel, did he reestablish his life on the foundations laid by Abraham and Isaac. Let's keep the faith; let's give our children "the truth, the whole truth, and nothing but the truth."

GOD'S WORD FOR ME TODAY IS . . .

Our methods may change, but our message never changes.

DAY 74

FREQUENT ENCOUNTERS WITH GOD!

These are the Scriptures that testify about me.

JOHN 5:39 NIV

Here are two compelling reasons for saturating your mind in the Scriptures: (1) To know who God is. One day in school, a little girl was asked by her art teacher what she was drawing. "A picture of God," she replied. The teacher said, "But nobody's ever seen Him." Confidently the little girl replied, "They will when I'm finished!" Till Jesus came, all we had were glimpses of God. Then Jesus announced, "He that hath seen me hath seen the Father" (Jn 14:9). If you want to know who God is, what He thinks and how He acts, start spending more time with Jesus. (2) To know who you are. When God called Moses to deliver Israel, Moses told God two things: (a) "When I . . . say to them, 'The God of your fathers has sent me to you,' and they say to me, 'What is His name?' what shall I say?' . . . God said to Moses . . . 'say . . . I AM has sent me to you'" (Ex 3:13-14 NKJV). In order to know who you are you must know who God is; then you'll have credibility, confidence, direction and purpose. (b) "'But suppose they will not believe me' . . . So the Lord said to him, 'What is that in your hand?' He said, 'A rod.' And He said, 'Cast it on the ground.' So he cast it on the ground, and it became a serpent" (Ex 4:1-3 NKJV). Moses already had what he needed, he just didn't recognize it or know how to use it until God showed him. Getting the idea? In order to know who you are and who God is, you must have frequent encounters with Him.

GOD'S WORD FOR ME TODAY IS . . .

If you want to know who God is, what He thinks and how He acts, start spending more time with Jesus.

DAY 75

READ YOUR BIBLE!

Your word is . . . a light to my path.

PSALM 119:105 NKJV

When asked, "What book has most influenced your life?" most folks say the Bible. Yet fewer than 14 percent of us read it every day. How come? Our most common excuses are:

(1) I've no time. Really? Many of the books in your Bible can be read in ten to forty-five minutes, some in less than twenty minutes. By taking a chapter a day you can complete the book of Proverbs in a month and the Epistle of James in five days. (2) I don't know where to begin. If starting in Genesis and working your way through seems overwhelming, break it into bite-sized pieces. Pick a Gospel and read the life of Christ. Just get started! (3) It's not exciting. Do you like romance? Read the book of Ruth. Looking for adventure? Try Judges or Acts. Enjoy poetry? Explore Song of Solomon. From history to how-to, it's all in Scripture. (4) Isn't going to church every week good enough? Billy Graham says, "The Bible is the road map for life, and while your pastor can highlight the best route to take, you learn how to navigate life's twists and turns for yourself." (5) It makes me uncomfortable. When you don't know what God's Word actually says, it's easy to equate it with negative experiences and hypocrisy you've observed, then throw out the baby with the bathwater. No question, the Bible makes you face hard truths. It "judges the thoughts and attitudes of the heart" (Heb 4:12 NIV). It gives you a checkup from the neck up. But you'll discover who you are, what you're called to do, and become empowered to do it!

GOD'S WORD FOR ME TODAY IS . . .

The Bible makes you face hard truths.

DAY 76

YOU MUST BE FAITHFUL

He was faithful to God, who appointed him.

HEBREWS 3:2 NLT

Faithfulness is more than just a nice concept; you must be faithful to something or someone. Actually, it's in making and keeping commitments to others that we demonstrate our faithfulness to God. "Whatsoever ye do in word or deed, do all in the name of the Lord" (Col 3:17). That means, to be seen by Him, to bring glory to Him, and to be rewarded by Him. If you don't love those around you, you don't really love God. Jesus put it this way: "Inasmuch as you did it to one of the least of these My brethren, you did it to Me" (Mt 25:40 NKJV). The Greek word for faithful means "to be trustworthy and reliable." When you give your word, can you be trusted to keep it? Many of us just aren't reliable. We can't be counted on to do what we say. It doesn't matter how gifted you are, if you're not trustworthy God cannot use you. And God will test you! How? By assigning you to do something for a period of time that you don't want to do, something that's not fun or exciting, something that may require you to submit to someone else's authority, something you chafe under. Then He will say to you, "Just be faithful." And faithfulness is not merely showing up day after day—it's showing up with a good attitude. God rewards that kind of faithfulness. Jesus said, "If you have not been trustworthy with someone else's property, who will give you property of your own?" (Lk 16:12 NIV). Simply stated—if you want to be successful, you must be faithful.

GOD'S WORD FOR ME TODAY IS . . .

It's in making and keeping commitments to others that we demonstrate our faithfulness to God.

DAY 77

STANDING WHEN EVERYTHING AROUND YOU IS FALLING (1)

Let him who thinks he stands take heed lest he fall.

1 CORINTHIANS 10:12 NKJV

Satan is out to tempt, trap, and topple you. Two of his favorite lies are:

(1) You can't fall. He appeals to your ego. "You've got your spiritual act together; you're too strong to stumble. Weaker people wouldn't be able to handle it, but you can." This lie is intended to make you overconfident, to lead you to "Trust in mankind . . . depend on flesh for (your) strength" and "turn away from the Lord" (See Jer 17:5 NIV). It's designed to get you to lower your guard and make you vulnerable to his schemes. Don't play into his hands! Be wise: "Pride goes before destruction, and a haughty spirit before a fall" (Pr 16:18 NKJV). Live on your knees. Fortify yourself with God's Word. (2) You can't stand. This appeals to your underlying sense of unworthiness, fear and inadequacy. He whispers: "Look at your track record. Compared to all those other good folks in church, you're not worthy to be called a Christian. Just give up." Satan wants to divert you from "Him who is able to keep you from stumbling, and to make you stand in the presence of His glory blameless with great joy" (Jude 24 NAS). He wants to get you focused on your negatives, your friends, spiritual giants who fell, and tell you that because they couldn't make it, you've no chance. He'll replay your list of shortcomings to discourage you. Don't go for it. "He is a liar and the father of lies" (Jn 8:44 NAS). Believing him makes you his victim. Refuse to let either pride or inadequacy defeat you.

GOD'S WORD FOR ME TODAY IS . . .

Live on your knees and fortify yourself with God's Word.

DAY 78

STANDING WHEN EVERYTHING AROUND YOU IS FALLING (2)

Let him who thinks he stands take heed lest he fall.

1 CORINTHIANS 10:12 NKJV

The truth is: (1) Standing isn't inevitable, but it is possible! The moment you commit your life to Jesus, you're at war with Satan. And standing up to him requires staying armed. "Put on the full armor of God, so that you will be able to stand firm against the schemes of the devil . . . that you will . . . resist in the evil day . . . and . . . stand firm" (Eph 6:11, 13 NAS). War is a casualty-laden business; you must take it as seriously as the Enemy does, for the Bible says he's out "seeking someone to devour" (1 Pe 5:8 NAS). Be alert, but not alarmed. "A thousand may fall at your side . . . but it shall not [happen to] you" (Ps 91:7 NAS). In conflict, some stand and some fall. The difference is, those who stand "have made the Lord . . . [their] dwelling place" (v. 9 NAS), whereas those who fall "make flesh [their] strength" (Jer 17:5 NAS). (2) Falling isn't always preventable, but it's surmountable! It's not only the weak and immature who fall. Satan's strategy includes taking out the righteous, the unrighteous, the most vulnerable and the least vulnerable—high-rankers included. "A righteous man falls seven times, and rises again" (Pr 24:16 NAS). Now if the righteous fall so frequently, what's to be anticipated from everyone else? In war no one is guaranteed immunity from attack. But, "A good man . . . Though he fall, he shall not be utterly cast down: for the Lord upholdeth him with his hand" (Ps 37:23-24). Don't focus on the unable, or the disabled—but on Christ the Enabler!

GOD'S WORD FOR ME TODAY IS . . .

In conflict, some stand and some fall. Those who stand "have made the Lord . . . [their] dwelling place."

DAY 79

BY GOD'S GRACE YOU'LL MAKE IT!

Out of weakness were made strong.

HEBREWS 11:34 NKJV

The Bible speaks of "Samson and Jephthah, also of David and Samuel . . . who through faith subdued kingdoms, worked righteousness, obtained promises, stopped the mouths of lions, quenched the violence of fire, escaped the edge of the sword, out of weakness were made strong" (vv. 32-34 NKJV). Who were these people? Jephthah, a social outcast born to an unwed mother. Samuel, a great prophet but not a great parent. David, who wrote many of the Psalms but had an affair. "Out of weakness were made strong." Notice, they didn't start out strong, they became strong. And if they can make it, you can too! For reasons God never explains, He chooses to work through people like us. He places us in difficult situations then unlocks our faith, compassion and creativity. When we don't know which way to go, He connects us with those who can open the right door at the right moment. Does that mean we won't experience fear? No, progress has always been made by people who faced their fears and rose above them. They knew that opportunity and security were opposites. The truth is, if the challenge you're facing doesn't place a demand on your faith, it neither pleases God nor involves Him. Phillips Brooks said: "Do not pray for easy lives; pray to be stronger people! Do not pray for tasks equal to your powers; pray for powers equal to your tasks. Then the doing of your work shall be no miracle, but you shall be the miracle. Every day you shall wonder at yourself, at the richness of life which has come to you by the grace of God."

GOD'S WORD FOR ME TODAY IS . . .

God places us in difficult situations then unlocks our faith, compassion and creativity.

DAY 80

IT'S A TEST OF FAITH

You . . . tested us . . . refined us like silver . . . [and] . . . brought us to a place of abundance.

PSALM 66:10-12 NIV

When Jesus explained the cost of following Him, some of His disciples walked away. Yet the impact of those who didn't is still felt in the world today. By the time they wrote their epistles, His apostles had learned to see every test in life as a chance to strengthen their faith and multiply their effectiveness.

Tests of faith are opportunities to surrender something of value to God, even when we have the right not to. In a test of faith you'll feel assaulted and stretched by circumstances, yet not distant from God; tried by them, but not judged or guilty. The Psalmist writes: "For you, O God, tested us; you refined us like silver . . . you brought us to a place of abundance." A test of faith doesn't really test anything unless it pushes you beyond your last test—past what you've already proven! If you try to run or pull back each time you reach what seems like your limit, you'll never know how much you can trust God—or how much He can trust you. The fire that refines us like silver can come as a job lost, a relationship lost, good health lost, or a reputation lost. But with God, the end result is never in doubt. If you're wondering today, "How much more can I take?" listen to the words of Bishop J. C. Ryle: "This only we may be assured of, that if tomorrow brings a cross, He who sends it can and will send the grace to bear it." In God's kingdom it works like this: "Faith tested, character refined, abundance given."

GOD'S WORD FOR ME TODAY IS . . .

Tests of faith are opportunities to surrender something of value to God.

DAY 81

IT HAPPENS TO THE BEST OF US!

These things happened . . . as examples.

1 CORINTHIANS 10:11 NKJV

A pastor was building a fence while the neighbor's twelve-year-old son watched. The pastor smiled and said, "Interested in carpentry, huh?" "Nope," the boy replied. "Just want to hear what a preacher says when he hits his thumb with a hammer!" You are the only Bible some people will ever read, and they're watching to see how your life lines up with what you profess. Some are hoping for confirmation of the life-changing power of Jesus, others for a chance to say, "See, Christians are all hypocrites!" We want to set a good example, but sometimes we fall short. And as humbling as it is to mess up, God uses those failures to "[make] it clear that our . . . power is from [Him], not . . . ourselves" (2Co 4:7 NLT). God doesn't glaze over the shortcomings of even the most notable saints. They're "all . . . written down so . . . we don't repeat their mistakes" (1Co 10:11 TM). Abraham, the "friend of God," lied about Sarah being his wife (See Ge 12:10-20). Moses, the mighty leader, got angry and disobeyed God (See Nu 20:1-13). David, a man after God's heart, committed adultery then tried to cover his tracks with murder (See 2Sa 11:5,15). Peter, head of the church, denied Jesus not once but three times (See Lk 22:54-62), and John Mark gave up and went with Barnabas to Cyprus (See Ac 15:38-39). They're all in there, warts and all, and Paul says, "We are just as capable of messing . . . up as they were" (1Co 10:12 TM). So don't get discouraged when you stumble. Admit your mistake, apologize to the people involved, ask God for forgiveness, forgive yourself, learn from what happened, and move on.

GOD'S WORD FOR ME TODAY IS . . .

You are the only Bible some people will ever read, and they're watching to see how your life lines up with what you profess.

DAY 82

BE DETERMINED!

Blessed is the man . . . whose confidence is in [God].

JEREMIAH 17:7 NIV

It takes courage to be led by God. It's not easy to "break the mold" and rise above the limits others place on you. When you do, you'll face disapproval. Jesus did. When the folks He grew up around said, "Isn't this the carpenter's son?" (Mt 13:55 NIV), they were really saying, "He should stay in His place!" When they tell you that, don't listen. "Each of us will give an account of himself to God" (Ro 14:12 NIV). In the final audit you'll discover that not only is it wrong to be judgmental of others, it's also wrong to permit their opinions to control you. "Blessed is the man who trusts in the Lord, whose confidence is in him." To follow God's leading you must have confidence that: (1) He loves you in spite of your shortcomings; (2) He has a definite plan for your life; (3) you are capable of hearing from Him for yourself; (4) whatever He asks of you, He will enable you to do. Once you've heard from God, be resolute! Things worth having never come easy. If you find yourself weakening, ask God for determination and He will impart it to you through His Spirit. If you find yourself being "double minded," go back and ask yourself what God told you in the beginning—then stick with it. Don't go in a different direction because of worry, or discouragement, or the sentiments of others. Remind yourself that you have what it takes to succeed in whatever God has called you to do. If you've made Jesus Lord of your life, His determination lives in you—because He lives in you.

GOD'S WORD FOR ME TODAY IS . . .

You have what it takes to succeed in whatever God has called you to do.

DAY 83

THE BENEFITS OF STRUGGLE

That you may be . . . fully developed.

JAMES 1:4 AMP

Overcoming obstacles is what develops in us the qualities we need to fulfill God's will for our lives. The truth is, it can't happen any other way. In Second Corinthians, chapter one, Paul spells out the benefits of going through hard times. Yes, there are actually benefits! Let's take a moment and look at some of them:

(1) "So that we will be able to comfort those who are in any affliction" (2Co 1:4 NAS). When people know you're qualified to speak, they listen. Otherwise, they politely tune you out. Built into every problem that forces you to grow, are the answers those around you need. When you can say, "I have been there," people respect you and pay attention. Experience is one of your greatest assets and God will use it. (2) "That we would not trust in ourselves" (v. 9 NAS). Anything that causes us to turn to God and lean harder on Him is an asset, not a liability. It's when we lose a job, a marriage, a loved one, our health, or our peace of mind that we turn to God and discover what He can do. (3) "That thanks may be given" (v. 11 NAS). Do you remember what your life was like before you met the Lord? The Psalmist wrote, "He . . . brought me up out of a horrible pit, out of the miry clay, and set my feet upon a rock" (Ps 40:2 NKJV). Come on, lift up your voice and begin to praise God for what He has done for you! After all, where would you be without Him? It doesn't bear thinking about—does it?

GOD'S WORD FOR ME TODAY IS . . .

Lift up your voice and begin to praise God for what He has done for you!

DAY 84

PUT GOD "FIRST" IN ALL THINGS

I require your . . . firstfruits.

EZEKIEL 20:40 AMP

God wants to be number one in your life! When He's not, things won't work out right for you. Instead of asking God to bless your agenda, ask Him to give you an agenda He can bless. Jesus was able to say yes to one thing and no to another because He understood God's agenda for the day. Can you point to a single stressed-out or confused moment in Christ's life? No, when conflict arose He said, "I do only those things which please the Father" (See Jn 8:29). That's because He took time to consult His Father. How long are you going to allow yourself to be pulled in 101 different directions? Nothing will change until you decide to give God what He requires—your "firstfruits." Don't give Him the part of your day when you're worn out, can't think straight and can hardly keep your eyes open; give Him the best part of your day. That's where your true priorities will be discovered. From getting dressed to setting your schedule, ask Him to help you make choices that glorify Him. As you become more and more aware of His presence, it'll be impossible to "compartmentalize" Him. Ordinary events will become sacred events because He's involved in them. Ask Him to direct you in the choices you make and to empower you for the jobs you need to get done. Keep Him first in everything you set out to do, and He will show you the path that leads to peace. Following the moment-by-moment leadership of the Holy Spirit will cause you to enjoy every day of your life.

GOD'S WORD FOR ME TODAY IS . . .

Ask God to give you an agenda He can bless.

DAY 85

REFUSE TO LET FEAR STOP YOU!

I was afraid.

LUKE 19:21 NIV

Ask yourself, "What would I attempt, if I weren't afraid of failing?" Jesus told of a man who entrusted his business to three key workers. He gave the first worker five talents, the second two, and the third one. In Bible times one talent was about fifteen years' salary, so you begin to grasp what an opportunity this was. It was a defining moment which gave each of them the chance to test their skills, develop initiative, practice good judgment, and profit from their investment. The first two men did exactly that, doubling theirs. But the third was afraid of failing, so he buried his talent. Jesus described this man as "wicked" and said his talents would be taken from him and given to the man who used his profitably. He wasn't judged for what he did, he was judged for doing nothing.

Fear of people, fear of failure, and fear of rejection can tempt you to bury your gift. Don't do it! Unless you've the courage to start—you're already finished. When God called people like Moses, Gideon, Deborah and Esther, they all had to overcome their natural fears; so will you. When they were in the wilderness, fear of lack made the Israelites want to go back to Egyptian slavery. Fear of persecution caused the disciples to forsake Jesus in His darkest hour, and caused Peter to deny Him—three times. Refuse to let fear stop you! How you use your talents is a matter of the utmost importance. The truth is, it's the basis upon which God will finally judge and reward you.

GOD'S WORD FOR ME TODAY IS . . .

Unless you've the courage to start—you're already finished

DAY 86

YOUR FAITH IS ON TRIAL

Do not think it strange.

1 PETER 4:12 NKJV

Faith in God doesn't exempt you from life's trials; it sustains you in them and grows stronger as a result of them. Trials come in different areas such as sickness, unemployment, relational conflict, and personal challenges. And trials have different time lines; some last a short season, others a lifetime. And trials, like storms, have different intensity levels. But most trials have one thing in common: they make you say, "If only I could understand why this has happened." The Bible answers this question in two Scriptures: (1) "Many are the afflictions of the righteous, but the Lord delivers him out of them all" (Ps 34:19 NKJV). (2) "For a little while . . . you have been grieved by various trials, that the genuineness of your faith, being much more precious than gold that perishes, though it is tested by fire, may be found to praise, honor, and glory" (1 Pe 1:6-7 NKJV). God is not Santa Claus or your bellhop. It's not His job to give you everything you want, exactly when you want it. Sure, God has promised to bless us, but when you major in "getting," by implication you question the faith of those who may not have as much as you. That's a mistake. Claiming God's promises doesn't mean you will escape adversity. Who told you that anyway? Not God! His Word says, "Do not think it strange concerning the fiery trial which is to try you, as though some strange thing happened to you." Real maturity often takes place in the crucible of pain. The truth is, you'll never know how strong your faith is till you've been there.

GOD'S WORD FOR ME TODAY IS . . .

Real maturity often takes place in the crucible of pain.

DAY 87

FURNACE FAITH

The God we serve is able to save us from it . . . But even if he does not.

DANIEL 3:17-18 NIV

Facing the fiery furnace, the three Hebrew children refused to compromise their beliefs or change their behavior. They told the king: "If we are thrown into the blazing furnace, the God we serve is able to save us from it, and he will rescue us from your hand . . . But even if he does not . . . we will not serve your gods." With the words, "even if he does not," they took their faith to a higher level. They knew God could prevent it, but not that His plan called for it in this instance. But they'd rather die than deny or disappoint Him. Understand this: God can take you out of your situation or bring you through it. When He leaves you in it longer than you'd like to stay, He's developing—furnace faith.

Furnace faith is dead to doubt and blind to impossibility. It reaches up through the threatening clouds and lays hold of the One who has all power in heaven and on earth. It makes the circumstances bearable and the future hopeful. Furnace faith believes that even if you do have to go through the fire, God will go through it with you. Listen to the words of a heathen king who watched it all happen: "I see four men loose, walking in . . . the fire, and they have no hurt; and the form of the fourth is like the Son of God" (Da 3:25). Furnace faith makes you as free in the fire of affliction as you are out of it. Furthermore, when your friends see the Lord in there with you, it'll convince them like nothing else.

GOD'S WORD FOR ME TODAY IS . . .

Furnace faith believes that if you have to go through fire, God will go through it with you.

DAY 88

STICK WITH IT AND YOU'LL WIN

His hand stuck to the sword.

2 SAMUEL 23:10 NKJV

Eleazar, one of David's "three mighty men," was the kind of person who wouldn't quit. When the Philistines attacked, we read: "Then the men of Israel retreated, but he stood his ground and struck down the Philistines till his hand grew tired and froze to the sword. The Lord brought about a great victory that day" (vv. 9-10 NIV). What a picture. "His hand stuck to the sword." Stick with it, and God will give you victory. When you give in to discouragement and quit, what more can He do for you?

Truett Cathy is not only a committed Christian, he's one of the world's most successful businessmen. He started Chick-fil-A with one small diner and it grew to more than 1,450 restaurants, making it the second largest quick-service chicken restaurant chain in America. As of September 2007, in Forbes Magazine's listing of billionaires, Cathy was number 380 in the United States with a net worth of 1.3 billion dollars. And this was achieved while remaining closed on Sundays, which is one of the busiest sales days of the week. In his autobiography he tells of being so tongue-tied he could hardly put two words together. Three weeks after he opened his first store it burned to the ground. When he finally got his second store, his brothers, who were his partners, were all killed in a plane crash. People advised him to quit. But instead he decided to trust God and keep trying. As a result his business employs thousands, and feeds millions every day. Truett Cathy took his setbacks and turned them into stepping stones. So, stick with it and you'll win.

GOD'S WORD FOR ME TODAY IS . . .

Stick with it, and God will give you victory.

DAY 89

TRUST GOD, AND DO SOMETHING!

Do not . . . be dismayed . . . I will help you.

ISAIAH 41:10 AMP

As long as you're willing to live with the problem, you won't solve it! Sometimes a situation that infuriates you, or unlocks your compassion, is a situation God's calling you to tackle. Nehemiah couldn't bear to think of Jerusalem in ruins, so he rallied God's people and rebuilt it. David, tired of Goliath's threats, put his life on the line and defeated him. Elijah couldn't tolerate idolatry so he took on the prophets of Baal, and won! If you're tired of the status quo, God may be calling you to change it. If so, He has promised, "Do not . . . be dismayed . . . I will help you." Henrietta Mears taught at First Presbyterian Church of Hollywood and influenced leaders like Billy Graham, Bill Bright, and former Senate Chaplain Richard Halverson. Disappointed by the lack of good educational material, she started her own publishing house—in her garage! Later it became Gospel Light Publications, one of the most effective in the world. When she couldn't find a good single-volume introduction to the Bible, she wrote one. To this day it remains a best-seller. Motivated by the lack of good retreat facilities for Christians living in crowded Los Angeles, she found the perfect spot in the San Gabriel Mountains. After praying in faith and negotiating, she got her retreat. It's now Forest Home, a top-notch conference center. Always, at the point of her greatest frustration, Henrietta would take a step of faith—and find a bridge was always there. In fact, on her deathbed, when somebody asked, "If you could do it all again, what would you do differently?" She replied, "I'd trust Christ even more!"

GOD'S WORD FOR ME TODAY IS . . .

Trust Christ even more!

Sept. 13. 2023

DAY 90

DON'T BE AFRAID; PUT GOD FIRST

I have commanded a widow . . . to provide for you.

1 KINGS 17:9 NKJV

When famine hit Israel, God said to the prophet Elijah, "Go to Zarephath . . . I have commanded a widow there to provide for you." Observe three things in this story: (1) When the need arises, your provision will be in place. That's how God works, so ask Him to tell you where to go and what to do. And when He does, get moving! (2) The people God uses will surprise you. Sometimes they're people you would tend to overlook. This penniless widow had "only a handful of flour . . . and a little oil" (v. 12 NKJV). That's no problem to God. He doesn't need much to start with in order to do something great, just a willing heart. Why didn't God send Elijah to a wealthy family? Because they didn't need a miracle, she did. When God's work has a need He looks for someone with a seed, stretches their faith, and both the giver and God's work are blessed. (3) Your "bad time" is often God's opportune moment. This miracle took place in the middle of an economic depression. What seems like the worst possible time for you, is when God loves to move. This woman was only one meal away from death; it doesn't get much worse. "So she went away and did according to the word of Elijah . . . she and . . . her household ate for many days. The bin of flour was not used up, nor did the jar of oil run dry" (vv. 15-16 NKJV). The key to her miracle is found in Elijah's words: "Do not fear . . . but make me a small cake from it first" (v. 13 NKJV). The Word for you today is don't be afraid; put God first and He will meet your need.

GOD'S WORD FOR ME TODAY IS . . .

What seems like the worst possible time for you, is when God loves to move

JOURNEY NOTES

JOURNEY NOTES

JOURNEY NOTES

JOURNEY NOTES

191

JOURNEY NOTES

JOURNEY NOTES

JOURNEY NOTES

JOURNEY NOTES

JOURNEY NOTES

JOURNEY NOTES

JOURNEY NOTES

JOURNEY NOTES

JOURNEY NOTES

JOURNEY NOTES

JOURNEY NOTES

JOURNEY NOTES

203

JOURNEY NOTES

JOURNEY NOTES

205

365 DAYS OF FAITH, HOPE & COURAGE

From the authors of
The Word for You Today

(Softcover, over 370 pages)

We all need a little faith, hope and courage to face the day. And some days, we need as much as we can get!

365 DAYS OF FAITH, HOPE & COURAGE is the perfect addition to your daily routine of spending time in God's Word.

Build up your faith, hope and courage each day. And when life's biggest challenges cross your path, you'll be ready to face them.

Order today:
wordforyou.com/fhc365
800.856.6159

(Hardcover, Over 250 Pages)

HE LOVES ME MOST

Experience God's Faithfulness Through Prayer

GET A COPY FOR YOURSELF AND ONE FOR A GIFT!

Packed with encouraging content and Scripture, this book is unlike any prayer journal you may have seen before. With more than 15 key topics that people struggle with at any given time, HE LOVES ME MOST guides you through Scriptures that will give you hope, help you engage with God through prayer, and experience a deeper relationship with Him.

And even in the best of times, staying close to Him is just as important. HE LOVES ME MOST will also walk you through those seasons where you can just be thankful and mindful of what He has done…just for you.

Order a copy for yourself and a friend.

Order today:
wordforyou.com/HeLovesMe
800.856.6159

Three New Releases in our Topical Book Series

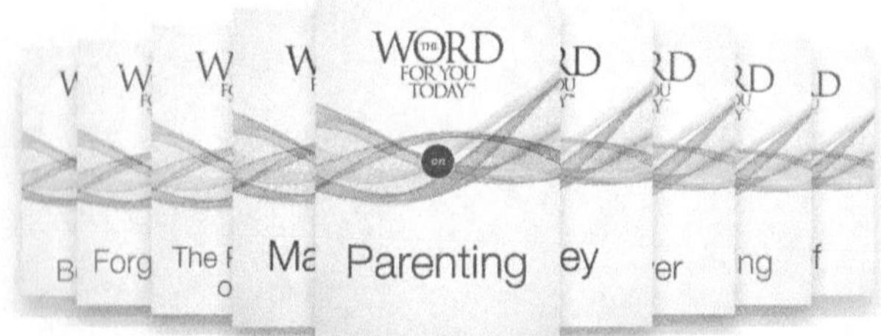

(Softcover, 80 Pages)

Our popular topical book series provides encouraging content and biblical insight on some of the most common issues we all face.

Topics include:

- Parenting
- Marriage
- Healing
- Forgiveness
- The Promises of God
- Money
- Prayer
- Grief
- New Believers

These little books are perfect for personal use or as gifts.
(Quantity discounts are available for larger orders.)

Order today: wordforyou.com/topics | 800.856.6159